You Can't Hide a
Dead Fish©

Cecilia Brown Thomas, M.Ed

You Can't Hide a Dead Fish©

Cecilia Brown Thomas, M.Ed

Copyright © 2014 Cecilia Brown Thomas

Published by 1st World Publishing
P.O. Box 2211, Fairfield, Iowa 52556
tel: 641-209-5000 • fax: 866-440-5234
web: www.1stworldpublishing.com

First Edition

LCCN: 2014954046
ISBN: 978-1-4218-8692-3

All rights reserved. No part of this book may be reproduced or utilized in any form or by any means, electronic or mechanical, including photocopying or recording, or by any information storage and retrieval system, without permission in writing from the author.

This material has been written and published for educational purposes to enhance one's well-being. In regard to health issues, the information is not intended as a substitute for appropriate care and advice from health professionals, nor does it equate to the assumption of medical or any other form of liability on the part of the publisher or author. The publisher and author shall have neither liability nor responsibility to any person or entity with respect to loss, damages, or injury claimed to be caused directly or indirectly by any information in this book.

CONTENTS

Introduction..........7
1. The Lost Boys..........9
2. Human Resources..........15
3. Parents..........25
4. Assessment..........37
5. Monsters, Bullies and Victims..........47
6. The Importance of Humor..........63
7. "Good" and "Bad" Schools and Teachers..........75
8. Hidden Treasures..........87
9. The Seamy Underbelly..........105
10. Racists, Pimps and Carpetbaggers..........117
11. Inspiration..........129

Introduction

"Educate and inform the whole mass of the people. Enable them to see that it is their interest to preserve peace and order, and they will preserve them. And it requires no very high degree of education to convince them of this. They are the only sure reliance for the preservation of our liberty."

—Thomas Jefferson to James Madison, 1787

The morning route to school was always the same. Travel several miles down the local turnpike, through the stoplights, over the marshy river where an occasional glimpse of a magnificent great blue heron served as my good omen for the day. Turn right into the neighborhood of modest, older homes; turn left onto the street that led to the school parking lot right after the house with the dog. There was that dog every morning, protected by the enclosure of his chain link fence; sometimes pacing around the yard, sometimes sitting still as a statue, always monitoring the passing cars. Usually he padded through the dewy grass, but every now and then he somehow managed to perch upon the top of his doghouse, surveying the broader vistas of his world and filled with confidence, no doubt, that he had it all figured out. I, the traveler, wondered about his life. I wondered what he had seen beyond this tiny plot of land and felt a little smug about the vastness of my perspective compared to his. He always inspired me to remember the greater possibilities.

This book is a journal of sorts; reflections upon my fifteen years as an elementary school counselor in two schools within a suburb of Richmond, Virginia as well as the ensuing years of involvement with the school system as an employer of teens and young adults. Someone recently asked me who would want to read this; who is the intended audience? I really thought about that. The audience, I hope, will be comprised of people who have an interest in the future of the American public school system; who believe that every human counts, that all children deserve a fundamental and appropriate education and that the cycle of despair and failure can be interrupted and rerouted at many junctures along the way. The people who embrace this book may come from all walks of life: elite and attendant, Bambi huggers and Bambi hunters, political activists who love this country but refuse to align with a particular party as well as those who do, the spiritually oblivious and the faith-filled. The stories, opinions and experiences relayed within the following pages may touch the conscience of leaders as well as ordinary citizens going about their lives. They may help people to remember that we are body, mind and spirit engaged in an ongoing struggle for internal and external balance. Or not.

I am the dog, you are the traveler. Even perched upon the roof of my doghouse I have a limited view of what goes on beyond the virtual fence around my own life experiences. Perhaps you will pass me by without a backward glance or, just maybe, my story will send you on an intriguing journey to the innermost core of your Self. I offer my words that you, too, may survey your own daily route and consider the greater possibilities. There are always greater possibilities.

Some names of people and places have been changed to protect both the innocent and the guilty.

Chapter 1
The Lost Boys

There can be no keener revelation of a society's soul than the way in which it treats its children.

—Nelson Mandela

April 1990

"Mrs. Thomas, this is Officer Johnson. I wanted to reach you before you heard it on the news… I know how concerned you are…"

"What is it?" I asked, and held my breath, unable to discern from his tone whether this would be good news or the worst.

"We think we've found the older one."

My mind screamed, *Well, why don't you ASK him?* even as I heard my voice whisper, "Is he… alive?"

"No, Ma'am."

I sank to the kitchen floor in a near faint, only vaguely hearing the gruesome details. His body had been discovered inadvertently, spilling out of a ripped plastic bag full of dirty diapers and garbage while being dumped into a landfill. His mouth and hands were bound with duct tape; his glasses neatly folded in his shirt pocket. At eight years old, he weighed all of 38 pounds. The younger brother was still missing. The search would continue.

How had it come to this? We had done everything right; that is, we had tapped all available resources to prevent it. Child Protective Services had been notified more than once about the physical and psychological torture, the systematic starvation even as the stepmother drove around in a car full of fast-food trash; the neglect, the public beatings and verbal abuse, the spying through classroom windows. They said they talked with the father and were assured that we "just didn't understand the Muslim religion." We said we had many Muslim families in our school over the years and this was not representative of their faith community.

We built a trust with the boys, encouraging them to relax and enjoy the safety of the school environment. The other students, many of whom looked forward to free lunch as their main meal of the day, slipped them part of their food when they noticed the brothers coming to lunch with only a book and a bottle of water. We secretly gave the cafeteria ladies a little money to provide occasional lunches for them, against the father's orders.

I had met with "Mr. M" alone once, asking him to help me understand his religion so that I could educate my co-workers. His dark, hate-filled eyes actually softened for a few moments as we had the only authentic dialogue in our history together; but his description of true Islam did not jive with the stark reality of his actions.

The police said it was a CPS issue, CPS said it was a religious matter, the Muslim community would not discuss it, mental health said they could not intervene in any situation where help was not requested by the people involved, the school administration said it was a CPS issue. Our fear for the boys intensified a little more each day. When Bahir told us in November that they would be moving back with their biological mother just south of the river, we rejoiced. He had never spoken ill of his father but quietly reported that he was "doing better" at times, allowing them out of their room for brief periods and even watching a little t.v. with them. The younger brother, Juhaym, was beginning to develop a persona similar to his dad's and was clearly the favored child. The stepmother, at nineteen, had a new baby and was obviously resentful of these children.

On their last day at Glenside I sat on the back steps with Bahir, telling him how very much I would miss him and hoped he would keep in touch. I encouraged him to introduce himself to his new school counselor and explained that she and I could send mail back and forth if he wanted to write to his classmates. He listened distractedly, far more interested in watching a group of disabled students play on the playground, and then turned to me with those beautiful, ageless eyes and said, "When I grow up, I want to work with kids like that. They need so much help." I put my arm around him and told him how lucky any child would be to have him as a teacher.

So how did it happen that on the first day of spring break, in April, we heard on the news that the boys had disappeared from their mother's home? We knew they would never go anywhere with a stranger as they were militaristically programmed to obey authority. The news gave a hotline number to call if anyone had information. I called and suggested that they were searching on the wrong side of town; that they would probably not find them near the mother's house, but near the father's. The detective responded with annoyance, "The father is helping us search, Ma'am." "I'm sure he is," I said, "but you're still searching the wrong area."

The assistant principal, Gladys, and I headed for the search site – a makeshift headquarters complete with volunteers, detectives, communication trailers and the crackling sound of police radios and walkie-talkies. In the midst of the activity was Mr. M, storming around with a look of grieved outrage, barking slanderously that the boys' mother had obviously not supervised them appropriately. Our eyes met and for an instant he froze. We walked toward one another and I hugged him, assuring him that all of us would do everything in our power to get to the bottom of it. He spewed more blaming judgment about his ex-wife and then disappeared back into the crowd.

Gladys and I spoke privately to a detective, providing the history of the family's time with us. He had already heard from our best friend and co-worker, Doris, who had taught both of the boys and shared the same details. We left the site spent and shaken.

That night I had the most incredible dream. I saw Bahir running through a field toward a big, hospitable farmhouse. He was smiling that brilliant smile and his little frame had plumped up from the tender loving care and sumptuous cooking of his new caregiver. On the wide front porch, surrounded by hand-woven rockers, flowers and baskets full of fresh vegetables yet to be canned stood a massive, aproned black woman. Arms opened wide, her resonant laughter emanated from the depths of her God-loving soul and Bahir giggled a muffled giggle as she smothered him in a huge, bosomy hug.

I woke up with a start, my heart filled with an inexplicable joy as the morning light streamed through a slivered opening in the bedroom curtains. I was certain it meant the boys had been taken by some loving relative; that, perhaps, their care was too much for the mom, and her extended family had stepped in to help as so often happens. It was a wonderful conspiracy, I thought; eventually, everyone would forget about their disappearance and they could live safely beyond the reach of evil relatives and bureaucratic nonsense.

I called Gladys and Doris with much excitement, convinced that I had been given some kind of a celestial glimpse into the truth of the matter. And when the phone rang that evening I jumped to answer it with almost mirthful anticipation, ready to feign distress as the search continued. And yet there I was, sitting on the kitchen floor with the cold, plastic phone to my ear, head spinning, wishing that this unthinkable news were the dream instead.

A huge body of incriminating evidence was found in Mr. M's basement including duct tape and diapers that matched the ones in the garbage bag containing Bahir's little body. Turns out that the bag originated in the dumpster near their house. Unfortunately, a local district attorney demanded that the public had a right to know what items were discovered and his hot-headed persistence damaged the case so that no arrests could be made. Juhaym was never found.

Some of us believe that Juhaym was not murdered at all but sent into some nefarious underground where he lives to this day. In any case, as of this writing the case is still considered open and no one has ever been charged. Bahir's brief time on this earth is neatly filed away among hundreds of other "cold case" folders. Whenever the grief and indignation sneak up on me, overwhelming me to tears, I remember the dream and offer up a prayer of gratitude. For now I realize that I was, indeed, allowed a privileged, celestial glimpse into his whereabouts.

Chapter 2
Human Resources

We always hope for the easy fix; the one, simple change that will erase a problem in a stroke.
But few things in life work this way. Instead, success requires making a hundred small steps go right – one after the other, no slipups, no goofs, everyone pitching in.

—Atul Gawande, *Better: A Surgeon's Notes on Performance*

The previous story incorporates many of the ongoing, challenging issues facing professional educators in the public schools. While the primary task at hand is to educate children, few people outside of the system recognize that we no longer live in that one-room-schoolhouse society where most children have two nurturing, biological parents tenaciously supporting the efforts of their teachers. Too many of America's children, across all socioeconomic lines, come from broken homes fraught with divorce, dysfunction, physical and/or psychological poverty and abuse; with transiency, lack of guidance and overall busyness of the adults whose job it is to mold them into healthy, productive members of society. So often people will say things like, "When I was a kid…" And when we were kids our own parents said the same thing, implying that the younger generation of the day was going to pieces. They were never right, until now. Sadly, much of the current, younger generation *is* going to pieces through no fault of their own.

Even when the story of "The Lost Boys" took place there was some semblance of order in families. Difficult kids and difficult parents in my county of employment were not the norm and could be approached on an individual basis as needed. But even then there was a limited network of support when crises arose and children who might otherwise have succeeded found themselves, instead, falling through cracks that would gradually expand into chasms. While the faith community of that father did not condone the behavior of their member, I wondered why no one among them had recognized the frustration level of this man and intervened at some point. Whether or not he and his second wife are actually guilty of the murder may never be determined but the torture and abuse were well known. The county's mental health agency made it clear that their services could only be engaged by the family itself. The Child Protective Service worker was young, inexperienced and naïve; her agency was tremendously short-staffed and underfunded as they covered not just our county but two adjoining ones as well. The police generally cannot become involved until after "something happens" and then it is too often too late and they are left to unravel and clean up everybody else's messes.

Unfortunately, things have not improved even with the passage of time. I served as an Elementary School Counselor from 1988-2003 and have remained in close contact with a number of my colleagues and students since I left. I have also continued to be involved with local schools and organizations that work with schools and, after leaving the system, I owned and operated a café with a staff of teens. If anything, the pressures and expectations imposed upon students and professional educators have become inversely proportional to the family and community support that is available beyond the classroom. One of the most abundant, available resources that could absolutely fill many of the gaps is the one most often overlooked and underestimated: human beings who care. I've often grumbled that if the people who criticize and condemn the school system would devote even a tenth of that passion toward actually rolling up their sleeves, traveling to a school of their choice and offering to *help*, it could change the world.

People tend to bemoan the situation with a dismissive, "But what can be done?" A more helpful question might be, "But what can *I* do?" Opportunities for simple yet profound interventions are endless, and even generational patterns of defeat can be broken. From womb to tomb we are all born, we live and we die. How we handle what happens in between is largely a result of imprints in the formative years unless stronger influences – for better or worse – shift us into different directions. Did we learn very early that the world is an unjust, dangerous place unworthy of our trust and compassion? Did our role models see themselves as victims or trailblazers? Did they nurture and encourage us or fill us with dread, fear and self-doubt? By the time we entered school our world view was already taking shape through the kaleidoscope of those early experiences. The good news is that even a minimal rotation of that scope changes everything! New shapes and colors emerge, our imaginations explode and the old configurations disappear. Contrary to popular belief, the efforts and policies that actually succeed in improving education do not necessarily need to take place exclusively within the school environment. People are everywhere. Regardless of race, culture or socioeconomic status we all have basic human needs as well as various levels of time, talent and treasures to share wherever we happen to be.

The following chapters will illustrate many of the triumphs and tragedies faced by families and educators every day. At the end of each chapter are general suggestions for anyone wishing to make a positive difference. Ideally these will serve as catalysts for your own creative ideas and actions, uniquely suited to your community. Every state, every county or city, even localities within counties and cities vary widely when it comes to policies, procedures, hierarchies of leadership and available resources with which to connect. As you read this book, jot down the "aha moments" that could later manifest into meaningful actions. Gently turn that kaleidoscope of your own perceptions and allow your world view to take on new dimensions. Everyday people are doing it every day, as illustrated below.

In the summer of 1992 I reconnected with a childhood friend who had become a successful motivational speaker and corporate team builder. In spite of a very busy schedule, he enthusiastically served on the board of a nonprofit organization called Volunteer Emergency Families for Children. VEFC was the brainchild of a small group of Presbyterian ministers who recognized the need for immediate placement of abused, abandoned or runaway children and youth at the onset of crisis. The organization had established a solid reputation for integrity, efficiency and success across the Commonwealth of Virginia. Now they were exploring the possibility of expanding their outreach to disadvantaged children who could benefit from tutoring and mentoring within the school setting. They already had a task force in place with every position filled except one: someone from the trenches, a professional educator to help them understand how to approach and work within the system.

Believing our meeting to be providential, my friend and I agreed to submit my name as a candidate for this spot. I had developed a similar program on a much smaller scale at Glenside and named it "BUOY" – an acronym for "Boosters Uplifting Our Youth" – in an effort to encourage local church and community involvement in our school.

In retrospect, I suppose the vision was somewhat grandiose for its time. While our school of about 350 students did have a handful of parent volunteers, I believed that elementary schools should be the nucleus of their entire neighborhood; of their designated zone. Every zone would be like the small town of old with spaghetti dinners and town meetings and adults who knew and cared about each others' kids. Even the adults whose children had long since left the nest – or who never had any at all – would be motivated to offer a friendly smile, a wave or a kind word to any child walking to and from school, crossing paths in the local convenience store or riding by on a bicycle. Preferably they would even know their names.

People from the community would turn out in droves for the PTA meetings, holiday programs, awards assemblies and such to cheer for the children – particularly those whose parents were unable or unwilling to attend. Everyone would clearly see the bigger picture – that kids who feel acknowledged and supported most often grow up with a sense of reciprocity, eager to tangibly contribute to the climate of peace and co-operation in their own communities. This, of course, would create a ripple effect of safe communities nationwide. Surely everyone who heard this idea would jump on the bandwagon!

I began by obtaining a list of every place of worship in our zone and added local day care centers in the hope that our students' caregivers might enjoy coming to some of the school activities. Over thirty letters went out to pastors, directors and youth ministers inviting them to an informational breakfast meeting just to brainstorm and become acquainted.

Sadly, fewer than one third of those who received an invitation took time to respond. Of those respondents, some said they could not come but would like to be kept informed and might consider becoming involved eventually. Some were not interested at all but several actually did show up – clearly the ones who were meant to be our new partners. Their eyes shone with expectation and the powerful sense of common purpose made us tingle as if connected by an electrical current. We chatted, snacked, toured the school, expanded upon the vision, shared logistical ideas for the program and committed to a second meeting as soon as I ironed out the details with school administration. Ultimately only two community leaders actually rose to the occasion, both Baptist ministers who rallied their members to commit. We were off to a shaky but enthusiastic start!

My friend Doris had become the assistant principal by then and she and I spent a few long days cleaning out a large "resource room" so the volunteers could use this space as well as the cafeteria and auditorium. We developed sign-in procedures, emergency cards, criminal background questionnaires, parent permission forms and packets of information with tips for working with students. The State Dept. of Volunteerism provided helpful information as well as the county itself. The ministers and their volunteers offered valuable and realistic suggestions about the shape and direction of the program.

Teachers were excited about enrichment opportunities for struggling students and readily submitted names and parental permission forms along with specific academic areas of need. Several shelves were sectioned off with teachers' names so the volunteers, once assigned to the students, could go to the spot and see what the teacher left for them in the way of instructions or resources. For volunteers who did not feel comfortable providing direct service to the children but were willing to help with clerical tasks there was more than enough work cutting, copying, laminating or organizing materials for the teachers.

While the little band of tutors and workers – primarily senior citizens – wasn't the multitude I had hoped for, their energy, devotion and reliability proved invaluable. We accommodated their schedules and soon the program took on a life of its own as these quiet angels came and went, signing in and out, working with individuals or small groups or pitching in on the mundane tasks at hand anywhere from an hour to three days a week. Any level of service was more than welcome and they had names of staff members to contact with questions or suggestions. The students were thrilled about the extra help and attention and teachers noticed improvement in both academics and behavior as confidence began to build and a sort of team spirit emerged. Although I continued to communicate with the broader group of church and child care directors by letter and phone, only the original volunteers remained committed on a regular basis.

Incidentally, there was never a conflict of interest between church and school, spiritual and secular. True people of faith never feel obliged to bludgeon people's sensibilities with words; they simply live what they believe even in the smallest acts of love known only to God, and hearts are changed forever. Even the ministers refrained from "preaching" – but they showed up if one of us picked up the phone and mentioned any kind of a crisis that could affect the children. Sometimes they would just eat lunch in the cafeteria, strategically placed to be a listening presence if desired. Sometimes they would actually visit classrooms with me, as when a teacher unexpectedly died on a Sunday night and her students needed to be informed the next morning, or when one of the students was shot to death as he walked home from the school bus. The students knew their faces and, even if they didn't want to talk, felt their compassion.

In 1997 there was a rather extensive shakeup in the personnel at Glenside and many of us were transferred to different schools. The building went into renovation, the administration changed and the BUOY program was abruptly discontinued.

I cherish the privilege of having witnessed firsthand how even a few caring human beings could make such a difference in this small setting. My belief in such effort was magnified after I became involved with Volunteer Emergency Families for Children and witnessed the impact of compassionate people on a grander scale. Fueled by their own zeal and with minimal input from me, that organization provided tutoring and mentoring programs in several "failing schools" around the state with incredible, documented results of success. I no longer need to wonder if tiny points of light might expand and impact the larger community when people answer the call. Although VEFC no longer exists, today there are many programs as large as theirs and as small as BUOY scattered throughout the darkness like stars on a moonless night. People of all spiritual perspectives have heard that same call, from the same Source, and regardless of their differences they seem to be guided by the same three internal, eternal forces of faith, hope and love.

Even in schools where volunteers are sparse or nonexistent there is usually an underground network of loving outreach as school personnel switch hats and go above and beyond to help the families they serve. As noted previously, efforts and policies that contribute to a successful school environment are not restricted to the brick and mortar of the school building. An entirely separate book could be written with accounts of quiet staff collaborations to collect and deliver food, money, clothing or Christmas gifts to those in need; of hospital visits, phone calls, well-timed hugs and tears; of connecting the dots of families to available community services; of faculty members cheering on their students at neighborhood sporting events and special ceremonies where there might be no one else who cared enough to attend. We usually only visualize a "ripple effect" as an outward force; but after the impact of stone to water the direction of the energy is actually a return to center. Try it and see. So it is with outreach. The ripples of a single touch expand beyond our limited gaze and then return in amazing and unexpected ways.

What can I do?

- Take time to assess your own gifts of stewardship – time, talent and treasure – to determine a personally satisfying and realistic level of commitment.
- Get to know your own community. What organizations, clubs or services directly benefit families and children, including schools and churches? Narrow down the list to those that resonate with your energy and interests. Just because you are "good at" something does not necessarily mean you enjoy doing it – follow your passion.
- If opportunities for outreach are limited, reinvent the wheel and start a program that has proven to be successful somewhere else. The gift of the internet is priceless.
- Volunteering does not necessarily require your physical presence. Monetary donations and supplies are always needed and welcome in schools and charitable organizations.
- Put down the phone, turn off the computer, take out the ear buds and make a conscious effort to become a familiar, friendly face in your neighborhood. Your compassion could save a life – maybe yours!

Chapter 3
Parents

Though no one can go back and make a brand new start, anyone can start from now and make a brand new beginning.

—Carl Bard

As with most grand ideas, the BUOY concept had sprung out of a desperate need. Our beautiful, bright-eyed youngsters were oblivious to their middle-to-low socioeconomic status, or the state of disrepair so common to old buildings or disparity of resources from one end of the county to the other. Like most kids anywhere they showed up on the first day of school excited about learning, wearing shiny new shoes and huge, irrepressible smiles with various stages of gaping holes as baby teeth surrendered to permanent ones. The teachers greeted them with warmth and enthusiasm, eager to hit the "restart button" and determined to provide whatever it took to help the kids succeed. But too often, like the innocence of baby teeth, the innocence of childhood was being replaced with a permanent feeling of inferiority and frustration as the odds stacked against them threatened to topple them altogether.

Again, through no fault of their own, many of the children were entering school way behind the starting line, so to speak. They lacked many of the opportunities for personal growth and academic enrichment that so many families take for granted.

While students at one end of the county might return to school in September rolling their eyes over the humdrum of having toured Europe during the summer, kids like ours were ecstatic if their day care had taken them roller skating or if they'd been allowed to spend a week in the country with Grandma – positive experiences to be sure, but limited.

The majority of the parents were very hard working, cared tremendously about their children's well-being and provided a modest but stimulating environment for them; but for many, paying the bills and putting food on the table had to take precedence over any frivolous extras. Very few sought or received government assistance, wishing instead to support themselves; and, in fact, few could have even qualified for such benefits with incomes that often set them just above the poverty line. They would come to school for conferences and events if possible but could not offer volunteer time or even receive phone calls if their jobs (sometimes several) involved shift work. Needless to say, students' grades and morale suffered from the repercussions of incomplete homework, unanswered communications from teachers and simple lack of follow-up to daily lessons that might not have been grasped the first time around.

In some cases the children of these folks were inadvertently neglected or even abused, but the parents were usually grateful for assistance. How could we fault the parents for their children's limitations when they were doing everything in their power to provide for their most basic needs? And how could we blame the children, who at least showed up every day with those beatific smiles and the willingness to try? The children and their parents counted on us to provide a well-rounded education and fill in the gaps as well.

Of course there were also parents at each end of the spectrum who were even greater cause for concern and exasperation. At one end were the purposefully abusive and neglectful, whose own psychological disorders determined their skewed priorities and life choices day after day. If the children in this group spoke at all about the situation at home it would be with much legitimate fear and trepidation about the consequences. They would quietly and sometimes accidentally reveal a precocious knowledge of sexual matters, or various extreme forms of corporal punishment, or illegal substances and weapons within easy reach. They regarded their parents with jumbled emotions: fierce protectiveness and revulsion, pride and shame, love and hatred, trust and skepticism. They fantasized that they were loved and nurtured by these adults who, in their minds, meant well and were unfairly blamed for any wrongdoings; but deep in their bellies they felt the constant, raw churning of fear and abandonment.

The manifestations of this ambivalence are as unique as the children themselves. While one might act out with outrageous, unacceptable behavior, another might be the perfect "teacher's helper." One might have failing grades while another makes the honor roll every time. A societal myth that schools must battle constantly is that abused and neglected kids are easy to spot and, therefore, a school psychologist or counselor can just zero in on "those kids" with therapies and community services without upsetting everybody else. The truth is, one should never presume to judge a situation by superficial evidence. The child who comes to school in the same outfit every day and receives free lunch may have an extended, loving family and all the right ingredients for success while the one who has all the latest trendy clothes and techno-gizmos may be resented, neglected and even tortured at home. A graphic example is the pattern of students involved in school shootings nationwide – too often, upper-middle class suburbia has produced the majority of these troubled youngsters.

Kids are encouraged to break the silence and believe that abundant resources will emerge from all directions. But they learn very early that any help of substance is minimal or nonexistent; that breaking the silence usually brings about consequences far worse than the original situation as social service workers declare their claims "unfounded" and leave them at the mercy of the perpetrators.

Early one morning I was on bus duty as usual, carrying my clipboard and checking off the buses as they arrived. *This is so pointless*, I thought. *The buses come, the kids flow smoothly into the building, the buses go – everybody knows the routine.* Cars were not allowed in the bus loop, as they dropped children at a different entrance. On this particular morning, however, a car pulled into the loop. A bus arrived behind it and couldn't release the students until the car moved. But the car just sat there, and no student emerged. Not being a perky morning person, I found this irritating. The bus drivers had a tight schedule and needed to proceed to the middle and high school runs, and a second bus was approaching the loop.

Assuming that some unruly child was refusing to get out while the parent coddled and cajoled, I approached the car prepared to fuss and move things along but a bizarre scene was unfolding. A very attractive, well-dressed woman was struggling to hold onto the steering wheel as an equally professional looking, handsome man seemed to be wrestling with her for control of the car, pulling at her hands and arms and pushing her into the door. The window was open and I instinctively shouted, "STOP that! What is GOING ON?" as if I were dealing with my own kids. The man looked up and his eyes met mine with an oddly sympathetic expression, conveying that this was a crazy woman and he was just trying to subdue her. Something just didn't feel right, though, and I gestured to the bus driver to call for help on her radio. As all the children watched, the car lurched forward in several small jerks, the driver's door flew open, the woman was thrust out onto the pavement and the car took off with the man at the wheel. He jumped the curb, peeled over the grass and then hit the road at top speed, disappearing in a flash.

I helped the woman to her feet and took her to a private room in the office where we assessed her for injuries and ensured her safety. Strangely, she didn't cry out or even say much of anything as the tears flowed and the police were called. By now the students who had been on the bus had spread word of the drama all over the school. We were concerned that the woman's three children would be worried so we gathered them from their classrooms and reunited them with their mom. Again, there was an incongruous air of calm as the mother assured them she was fine and sent them back to their classrooms. Two boys and a girl, these were model students who did well academically and never called attention to themselves with misbehavior.

As the police arrived to question the woman, one went into the room and shut the door while the other asked to use the office phone. My knees buckled as I overheard the gist of his conversation with words like "wanted felon", "has been on the run", "record of violence" etc. Just minutes earlier I had been outside shaking my finger in the face of a violent criminal and yelling at him like he was a five-year-old! I had to sit…

It turned out that this man had been in the school earlier that morning briefly visiting his children's teachers and never raised a moment of suspicion. He then went out to the parking lot, hid among the parked cars and waited for his estranged wife to drop off the kids at the correct entrance and then jumped into the passenger side of the car and demanded that she drive. She wisely pulled into the bus loop knowing that it would draw attention. Before she left we told her not to hesitate to have us subpoenaed if this went to court and they needed witnesses. She graciously thanked us, arranged transportation to get to work that day and unceremoniously left the school.

Months passed before the man was captured and a court date was set. The bus driver and I were subpoenaed and we were eager to testify on behalf of this mother and her kids. When the day arrived we sat together in the waiting area outside the courtroom as the social workers, lawyers, deputies and other legal professionals went behind closed doors for a preliminary meeting. We saw the mother sitting alone and went to her to tell her again that we would do whatever was necessary to help. She was nervous, yet quiet and composed, clearly not wanting to talk, so we left and sat elsewhere. Soon she was called into the courtroom and we waited. And waited...

After awhile the door opened and all of the people spilled out except the mother, who apparently left through a different exit. As everyone began to scatter in different directions we stopped someone and asked, "What happened? Weren't we supposed to testify in this case?" The jaded case worker responded matter-of-factly, "She didn't press charges. She said she isn't afraid of him, has never been afraid of him, and it was all a misunderstanding. He'll be tried for other offenses but this one has been dropped." Like our jaws.

But now it all made sense. The calm façade masked a deep, pervasive terror. There was no way this woman could have spoken against this extremely dangerous man. She feared for her life and the lives of her children and they, too, had learned to be strong and invisible. Bad people don't stay in jail, and even if they do there are "associates" who will take care of business on the outside. Restraining orders mean nothing; fear and obedience save lives, sometimes. Real, guaranteed help is not available and breaking the silence can be deadly.

But again, who is to blame? The helping agencies whose budgets and personnel are always the first to be cut in a slow economy? The back-logged court system that has too little help and far too few facilities for incarceration and/or programs for rehabilitation? The limited shelters for victims of domestic violence? The public too often sits in coffee-sipping comfort over the morning paper, railing in judgment against the inadequacies of others with the shades drawn, doors bolted and finances in a personal feedback loop. Sometimes just one person in the right place at the right time can be as vital as a railway switch, shifting a life from one track to another at a critical junction. How often do we read stories of great people who overcame seemingly insurmountable odds because of one person who cared or took a chance on someone along the way?

At the other end of the spectrum from the blatantly menacing adults are the parents who are disconcerting in a different way. Their children are *never* at fault and they hover, blame, threaten lawsuits and demand to be in control of every detail of the school experience because they clearly know more than a bunch of silly teachers. Like the neglectful and abusive ones, they cross all socioeconomic lines and ultimately prove to be the greatest handicapping condition the child might ever have. These same parents are shocked and defiant when, eventually, their young adults engage in illegal activities or simply fail at life, having developed no life skills or sense of personal responsibility beyond their own wants and needs. They feel entitled for one reason or another and the array is amazingly wide. For some, a victim mentality has been perpetrated for generations and they, therefore, vehemently believe that the world owes them everything with no effort required on their part. Others demand special treatment for their children because they, the parents, have this or that job or income or "connection" to influential people. My friend Gladys, who eventually became the principal of a very affluent elementary school, tells of a parent who was in her office sobbing hysterically because her child, after a series of academic tests, had not qualified for the "gifted" program. Gasping through the tears, she choked out, "But we live in the gifted *neighborhood!*"

In a perfect world parents and educators would be respectful, collaborative allies and advocates for *all* children. People would pay attention to the school curriculum as it is developed and express concerns and positive suggestions before any programs become permanently embedded. Local leaders would be carefully vetted, elected and held accountable in their leadership roles. Responsible parents of successful kids would reach out to those less equipped for child rearing by supporting a strong and active parent-teacher organization and creating or partnering with programs that provide parent education and support. The community would provide safe houses for those in danger and mandatory sentencing for violent criminals. And in systems where there is glaring disparity of resources, an independent, charitable organization would be established where people could contribute supplies or funds to fill the gaps. As wonderful as Goodwill, Salvation Army and such organizations are, it would be nice if generous donations of goods, services and money could be centrally located and managed specifically within and for a school system, with customized lists of needs shared with the local residents. The utilization of social media and basic technology would make it simple and cost-effective. Even in an imperfect world these are not unattainable goals.

The nomenclature of "parent" really is a title that should be earned and not automatically acquired upon the birth of a baby. True parents come in many colors, shapes and sizes and are not necessarily biologically connected to the little souls in their care. Honestly, the fact that two human beings can mate and produce a baby does not suddenly transform them into Mary and Joseph. They are who they always were except suddenly they bear the awesome privilege and responsibility of shaping the life of another. Whether we like it or not, in this day and age of family transiency and dysfunction it *does* take a village to raise responsible, productive citizens and the neighborhood school is the logical center of the village. There is no more essential investment in the future than the emotional, physical, intellectual and spiritual nurturing of all children so that, ideally, when the day comes for them to leave the nest they will be fully armed – not with weapons, but with the elements of knowledge and good character.

This is certainly not a new idea. St. Paul encouraged the Galatians similarly: *My brothers, if someone is detected in sin, you who live by the spirit should gently set him right, each of you trying to avoid falling into temptation himself. Help carry one another's burdens; in that way you will fulfill the law of Christ.* (Gal. 6:1-2)

One morning I was wrapping up a series of weekly sessions with a group of fifth grade boys who had been referred by their guardians for help in dealing with divorce. Several of them were already headed for trouble and liked to appear tough in their own worlds, but in this environment they had dropped their false personas and felt comfortable speaking from their hearts. I asked the question, "When you think about your future, what do you wish for?" The first one said, "I wish I could live a long life and die of natural causes." They all nodded in agreement. Another said, "I want to have at least one child before I die. A little girl." This time they emphatically agreed – looking at one another and, again, nodding their heads.

It occurred to me that most ten and eleven year olds believe themselves to be immortal and invulnerable, wishing for a life filled with adventure, prosperity and great accomplishments bordering on super-hero status. These young men, however, felt destined for a short life. Sudden death was commonplace in their experience and too few had a father or stable male role model to guide them otherwise. The mothers of children like these often resented the absent fathers, passing along the subliminal and sometimes outspoken message that *men are bad, men are unreliable, men are inadequate,* etc. To a little boy who has no comparative references, this translates into ***I am bad,** unreliable, inadequate...* And so they wish for a legacy that is good; proof of their existence, an innocent child, preferably a girl, as girls are *good*.

I had some little end-of-the-group gifts for them, one of

which was a bookmark with the words of the 23rd psalm. While I never preached to my students, I did feel free to share what seemed to work for me and in so doing often discovered the children, too, had deeply held spiritual beliefs that they kept to themselves. I offered a little disclaimer before handing out the bookmarks, saying that they could choose not to take one but that I wanted to read the words to them before they decided. I began, "The Lord is my shepherd, I shall not want…" A quiet voice merged into mine, "…He maketh me to lie down in green pastures…" One by one, timidly stealing glances back and forth, each of them began to join in until we were reciting the entire psalm in unison, "…surely goodness and mercy shall follow me all the days of my life, and I will dwell in the house of the Lord forever." Then silence. Permeating peace as, for one perfect moment, we all shared a sense of unconditional love, hope and oneness. I mentally thanked the adults who referred them to this group, real parents who were clearly doing the best they could. The boys each took a bookmark and I told them I looked forward to hearing the wonderful, scriptural rap music they would one day perform! Laughter, hugs, and they were gone.

What can I do?

- If you have successfully raised children of your own, share the wealth! Is there a program in your community that needs help with classes for teen mothers? Are there support groups where frustrated parents can go for understanding and practical, compassionate advice from others who have "been there"? If not, start one!
- An inadequate academic foundation is often the root cause of poverty. Are there organizations that welcome guest speakers, tutors or mentors for high school dropouts who would like to earn their G.E.D? Begin by checking with the community colleges and technical centers. Even if they don't need help they will be able to direct you to other agencies or organizations that would appreciate your assistance.
- If you have no children of your own but long to share the love in your heart, consider becoming a foster parent. According to the U.S. Dept. of Health and Human Services "AFCARS"* report ending in September of 2012, there were 397,122 boys and girls in foster care in this country. All of them dream of that "forever family" but hope, at the very least, for even a temporary experience of family love. *(Adoption and Foster Care Analysis and Reporting System)
- If a child or an adult "breaks the silence" with you, do you know what kinds of resources are available? Do some research on your state and local domestic violence programs so you will be in a position to offer meaningful help.
- The Boys and Girls Clubs of America are always seeking mentors, especially males. If there is no chapter in your locality, start one!

36 | You Can't Hide a Dead Fish

Chapter 4
Assessment

It is not sufficient, and it may actually undermine our democracy, to concentrate on producing people who do well on standardized tests and who define success as getting a well-paid job.

—Nel Noddings

The passionate outcries were familiar. The torrent of indignation after the long, silent tension was as predictable as raging floodwaters after snow-capped mountains begin to thaw.

"The questions are confusing!"

"I KNOW this stuff, but I don't know what they're ASKING!"

"There could be a LOT of answers to some of these questions!"

"I wouldn't have picked ANY of the answers on some of them!"

"There should be some way to EXPLAIN an answer!"

"I can't believe that something like this can determine relicensure!"

Relicensure? My brain began to regroup… My ears heard the voices of my elementary school students after every standardized test. My heart deeply felt their pain and frustration. But my eyes saw a group of grown men and women – physicians – justifiably respected in their fields; competent, confident, highly educated.

Yet here they were, feeling powerless and resentful; desperately wanting to prove they did, in fact, know the required material and were, indeed, worthy and able to do what they did every day for a living. This was my husband's lunch break during the American Board of Family Physicians boards (before the days of online testing) required every six years throughout the professional lifetime of a Board Certified Family Physician. They truly were the experts, successful and ethical and deserving of a more reliable assessment tool than this one test.

Tentatively, I submitted, "Our society places a lot of trust in the validity of standardized tests. It doesn't occur to most people that the instrument itself might be flawed."

I was met with annoyed looks as they continued to lament. I quietly persisted, "How will you feel if there's a low pass rate and the media starts blasting Family Physicians as being incompetent?"

"They won't," someone responded. "The ABFP will study the exam, throw out any questions that were clearly ambiguous and welcome professional feedback about the test so that it can be improved."

"In the school system," I offered, "if children do poorly on a standardized test the media criticizes and humiliates the teachers and publishes the scores in the newspaper. And the children feel stupid, develop test phobia, and eventually lose any enjoyment of the learning process. Some of them have a knack for objective tests, but a lot of them need to demonstrate their level of understanding in other ways..."

"I HAVEN'T BEEN A CHILD FOR 50 YEARS AND THAT HAS NOTHING TO DO WITH ME!" the Most Belligerent One interrupted. I retreated back into the sanctuary of my thoughts and observations, just as my students did when they believed they had just said the dumbest thing ever.

How do we build bridges between the young, vulnerable learners who do not yet have concrete evidence of their intelligence – the diploma, the degree, the successful career – and the veteran learner who can thumb his nose at a test and maintain some sense of intellectual proficiency? If a test can so adversely affect a group of professionals who prove themselves on a daily basis, what must the effect be upon those who are just beginning to tiptoe into the world of information; who may have any number of methods of assimilating and communicating that information but not necessarily through the medium of a standardized test?

Bright, even gifted kids may be denied full diplomas if their abilities do not register on a state-sanctioned test. Innovative, dedicated teachers may be able to show documentation of student progress in leaps and bounds, but individual progress is not as valued as the comparison of large, unrelated groups to one another. Some statewide tests are not even normed by a given population before being fully implemented and utilized for comparative purposes. And the curriculum for such tests is often developed long after the test itself, resulting in a huge disparity of resources and materials among localities who are then judged with equal expectations.

In most communities the verbal bantering on this issue happens primarily among parents, politicians, media and professional people outside the field of education who fiercely believe that expertise in their fields qualifies them as experts in the field of education. The voices of the educators themselves will generally go unheard unless they fully support the local party line; public disagreement is viewed as a negative attitude, and careers abruptly end as a result.

But all is not lost! Children are naturally curious, eager to please and highly responsive to positive methods of gauging their progress. If we truly wish to sow the seeds of yearning for lifelong learning in our children, we must begin by recognizing that teaching and learning are like an intricate, lovely dance where the partners take turns leading and following. We live in a time of information overload and the daily development of new bells and whistles for accessing data. Research development and available results – including brain research – are eons ahead of the questions asked and the tools that measure mastery. Students are often more technologically sophisticated than their parents and teachers and can come up with incredible ways of exhibiting their knowledge when given the opportunity. The memorization and regurgitation of disconnected info-nuggets is beyond old-fashioned; it is irresponsible, and irrelevant to the development of an informed citizenry.

Obviously, at the primary levels children must learn basic reading, writing and math skills in order to transition successfully through the entire educational experience. Memorization is vital when one is learning to count, or recognize letters, or develop handwriting ability. But I wonder if a second-grader really needs to spew out facts about the pyramids and pharaohs of Egypt when he or she does not yet comprehend the difference between a neighborhood and a nation?

It would behoove state-level and even central office administrators, as well as teacher educators, to return to the classroom as full-time teachers every so often after they leave the local school level. It takes about five years away from the trenches, in my estimation, to totally lose touch with the reality of the day-to-day issues educators face. And teachers should be given opportunities to rotate through administrative positions to garner a better understanding of the challenges and pressures at the top. The morale of a faculty absolutely sets the tone of the learning environment, and students who face depressed, resentful teachers every day are not likely to bubble over with enthusiasm or motivation to do their best. Teachers and administrators who work collaboratively, with a healthy appreciation of each others' roles, contribute to a level playing field for students.

But what of the testing process itself? In this national climate of data-driven, high-stakes testing, is it possible to humanely generate meaningful results without slaughtering the spirits of our young people? Absolutely, but the task must be entrusted to the parents and professionals and not the peanut gallery.

Most states have the opportunity to come up with their own assessment tools as long as there is resulting data that can be compared and contrasted as evidence of achievement. In Virginia, this K-12 "package" is known as the Standards of Learning, or SOLs. State-generated tests are administered at certain grade levels, with comparable division-made tests for the alternating ones. At the elementary level some other tests given throughout the year include tests of phonetic awareness, general ability tests, achievement tests and all of the usual tests and quizzes created by teachers. All of the assessments are important, but none is subject to the same level of scrutiny, security, foreboding and dire repercussion as the SOL test. The results of this instrument determine school accreditation, staff reputation, job security, and even real estate values!

As more and more schools become "accredited" in Virginia people should be asking what that status means, exactly. Are there truly meaningful, long-term ramifications to the successful parroting of SOL material? Does achievement on an SOL test translate into achievement on tests that are nationally accepted as valid and reliable? Do the high-scoring students fare better in the workplace, or in life? Are they demonstrating evidence of improved citizenship and character? By graduation, do they have a good understanding of the history of their own nation and its role in the bigger picture of the world? Or are they only able to describe and define those people and points that were selected for The Test?

As the physicians realized, information is a moving target of sorts. Far more important than bubbling in a sheet of facts that may or may not make them good doctors is the ability to stay current; to know how to access a multitude of resources and change their methodology with the changing information. Accountability and expertise should be measured by more than one tool, and the tools should be vetted and relevant. Seems like common sense. In the case of school children, narrowly defined test results often do not illustrate an accurate learning profile and yet they profoundly affect students' future academic direction. While doctors have feedback on their success or failure through patient recovery or lack thereof, school children have no other recourse to prove themselves.

For example, an "ability" test purports to measure achievement potential; even intelligence itself. But, with the exception of brief directions that may be read by the teacher at the onset of the test, the child must often read the test in its entirety. If reading is an area of difficulty, then this weakness will negatively impact all subject areas across the board including mathematics since "quantitative" tests include word problems, and directions-within-the-directions that explain each section. A child with reading problems cannot possibly do his or her best if the teacher is not allowed to help with a word or a phrase that explains what to do, and rephrasing a question for clarification purposes is absolutely forbidden.

Some ability tests include "language arts" sections that are nothing more than big vocabulary tests. There might be a question with three or four pictures from which to choose a correct response, and neither the question nor the pictures are clear. One of my personal favorites was on a first grade, nationally standardized test. There were four sketches of generic, four-legged animals and the question asked, "Which one bleats?" Even if the child knew what "bleats" meant, he then had to figure out what kinds of animals the pictures were trying to represent! Another asked, "Which is the largest?" and showed figures of different sizes. An incorrect response can be the result of a dialectical glitch in which the child customarily says "biggest" to describe largeness and does not understand the question.

If those who are obsessed with meaningful data genuinely wanted to assess student knowledge they would create no-nonsense, straightforward instruments that allowed every opportunity for success. There would not be ridiculous security requirements with everyone in the building signing contracts where they swear never to reveal anything on the test, or special rooms and vaults where the materials are kept under lock and key, or "irregularity" forms that must be submitted to the state if a child interrupts the test or vomits from the stress.

During one of these grueling testing episodes, a very bright, fifth grade male student had explosive diarrhea at the completion of his exam. The teacher quietly sent a courier to my office with a sealed note asking if I could figure out a way to remove the ailing student from the room before the other children realized what happened. I sent the little messenger back – with a similarly sealed response – suggesting that the teacher write a bogus note for the sick child to take to the clinic at which time the school nurse and I would talk to him and call his mom for a change of clothes. Upon intercepting him at the clinic I gently asked the child, "Did you have a little accident?" He looked at me with a confused expression and said, "No." I reframed... "Is your stomach upset?" Even more confused, another, "No." I realized at that moment that this child was stressed to the point of total *dissociation* – he honestly *did not know* that he had lost bowel control. His mother showed up with a change of clothes and went into the clinic bathroom with him but then came out and reported that she would actually have to take him home. The gravity-defying diarrhea had shot up his back, soiling his pants, shirt and torso to the extent that he would need to totally strip down and shower in the privacy of his home. But he did not know. Really. Fortunately for his teacher, he had already turned in his test; otherwise, she would have had to declare a testing "irregularity" which, after all, is the more important issue in a case like this. And fortunately for him there was a compassionate, experienced teacher who probably saved him from a lifetime of teasing.

I believe that each grade level should be given a pre-test in the fall that's almost a duplicate of the "real thing" that will be administered in the spring – after the subject matter is actually *taught* – so true progress can be measured. Tricky questions should be eliminated altogether – we are not, after all, trying to weed out incompetent brain surgeons at this level! We are simply trying to find out if the children learned what we hoped they would learn between September and June. And what they learn should be relevant and developmentally appropriate.

Assessment obviously must include objective, standardized types of tests but should definitely also include subjective measurement involving writing, oral response, projects, class work, teacher-made tests and even technology with assistance provided as needed. Students with reading problems should be allowed to have confusing parts read to them in any test other than an actual reading test where the frustration level obviously does need to be measured in order to be remediated. Schools in socio-economically disadvantaged areas should not be mocked and punished because their scores are lower due to a lack of funds or enrichment resources – human and otherwise – that other schools enjoy. A commitment must be made at all levels, public and private, to fill the voids wherever possible if the comparisons are to be fair and meaningful.

Nothing kills a love of learning faster than a feeling of personal inadequacy. Using standardized tests as the sole means of evaluation is a surefire way to drown out any sparks of enthusiasm for learning or teaching. As beautiful, complex beings who embody enormous and infinite gifts of body, mind and spirit, can we truly be defined by such one-dimensional instruments? And, ethically speaking, should we?

What can I do?

- Explore your state Department of Education and county/city websites to learn about the curriculum, assessment tools, materials and expectations for academic success at each level. This is public information. If anything seems unclear, unfair, unrealistic or unconstitutional, make your concerns known to local leaders.
- Attention Deficit (Hyperactivity) Disorder, while not addressed in this chapter, is grossly misunderstood and can actually determine a student's success or failure when misdiagnosed – especially when it comes to testing. If you volunteer as a tutor or mentor you will inevitably encounter children who have difficulty with focus and concentration. Educate yourself about this subject as much as possible ahead of time.
- If you have chosen to home school your own children, make sure that your program prepares them for the kinds of tests required to qualify for a recognized high school diploma or college admission exams.
- Attend school board meetings to see what the priorities and challenges are. Offer your educated, respectful and positive suggestions whenever possible. Never assume that your ideas will be dismissed by the professionals.
- As stated previously, every jurisdiction has its own unique policies, procedures and hierarchies even within the same state. If a school requires something that simply does not "pass the smell test" for you, take time to explore the source and justification of that requirement and call public attention to it if necessary.

Chapter 5
Monsters, Bullies and Victims

The world is a dangerous place, not because of those who do evil, but because of those who look on and do nothing.

—Albert Einstein

During my first year as a counselor, Shante was referred to me because of a stash of inappropriate drawings she had shared with her friends. The anatomical depictions were only as accurate as her nine years of life would allow, but the activities being portrayed were quite clear – oral sex, intercourse and fondling in a variety of situations with one or several people. My job was supposed to be disciplinary in nature – Shante found the whole thing pretty amusing and said she saw these images "in a magazine." Something deep in my gut told me this was not the case; something about her overall behavior was incongruous with the typical interactions of a child her age. We chatted, played a little, and talked more about the drawings. Eventually the bravado melted into a gentle flow of tears as she confided that her uncle had been doing those things to her and her older sister. My inner, sword-swinging warrior galloped to the surface on a mighty steed as I promised to help her and assured her that she had done the right thing in speaking out.

I met with her sister, a fifth grader at the same school, and only with encouragement from Shante did she verify that this was true. They had been forbidden to discuss it by Uncle Hugh; their mother had dismissed it altogether when they tried to confide in her.

I reported the situation to a weary Child Protective Services worker who said she would try to send someone out as soon as one of the case workers had an opening in the schedule. Eventually a case worker did show up – a male, with a male detective from the police department – and I was not allowed in on the discussion. I knew the girls would be very uncomfortable talking with anyone about this, particularly males, but I was grateful that the "professionals" were at least in the loop.

For the next several months the girls were in and out of meetings with various people and neither of them seemed interested in talking with me again. While it was disturbing to know that they were going home to the same circumstances day after day, I figured the courts or social services had assigned them to a counselor and that was fine; surely they were being nurtured through the system and empowered to speak up truthfully in court.

Months passed and finally Shante left a note in my box requesting a visit. When she arrived she was scared, ashamed, and filled with enormous guilt and regret for having talked to me. All of the adults in her family, including her mother, were agonizing over "poor Uncle Hugh" because he might have to go to jail and it was all Shante's fault. They repeatedly reprimanded her for telling on Uncle Hugh and involving her sister in the session, and her cousins berated both of them for getting their daddy in trouble. I did my best to assure her that she had made a good choice; that Uncle Hugh, not she, was responsible for whatever decision the court handed down. He was the one who made a bad choice. She agreed but still felt heavily burdened by the huge battle within the family and believed she should have kept quiet.

The day in court came and went and Shante gave me a brief

summary of the proceedings. She and her sister were forced to sit on the witness stand in front of everyone in the family – including Uncle Hugh – while attorneys assaulted these little girls with the most intimate, humiliating questions imaginable as everyone glared disapprovingly. They could not speak. They could hardly breathe. All charges were dropped. They did not wish to see me or anyone else ever again about this matter. They had learned their lesson.

Mickey was a sweet, red-haired-freckled-face fourth grader whose teacher was frustrated with him because he absolutely refused to do any work. He was obviously quite intelligent – always scored well on the sacred standardized tests, spoke articulately and with a quick, endearing smile. He was older than the other kids in his class, having already been retained once for failing grades, and he was heading for another retention as the F's accumulated on the report card once more.

At the request of his mother and his teacher we set up a regular, weekly time to meet. During those meetings he drew wonderful pictures, wrote in a journal, chatted freely and totally captured my heart. Many branches of his family were filled with problematic issues – alcoholism, child abuse, divorce, biological parents moving in with step-parents and children when their lives came crashing down. But Mickey planned to beat the odds – he had big dreams, loved to work on cars, read well and hoped to have a life one day with a "nice, pretty wife and some kids."

Fourth grade silently slid into fifth and Mickey was a tall, maturing twelve year old adolescent among ten and eleven year olds. He was still unmotivated academically but poured out his heart and demonstrated his talents one-on-one. I tried unsuccessfully to find any local mechanics who might be willing to take him on as sort of an apprentice; everyone feared the potential liability of having someone that young in their shops. I told his mother about various opportunities for him to get involved with healthy clubs or groups in the community but transportation was always a problem. He actually longed to go to church. I called several in the area to see if they had any kind of a system in place to transport youth but, again, the liability issue of shuttling kids from their homes to church and back without parental supervision was too frightening.

The local mental health agency had been involved with their family for years but compliance was always an issue and appointments were constantly missed. Mickey shared that he was very worried about the safety of his cousin, who attended another school, because the boy's father (Mickey's uncle) beat and abused him relentlessly and had landed him in the hospital more than once. I phoned the counselor at his cousin's school as well as the mental health counselor, but everyone said that unless the boy came forward with this information himself there could be no intervention.

We put Mickey through a full evaluation process to see if he qualified for any services through the Exceptional Education department and did find that he qualified for an Individualized Education Program – or "IEP" – with a label of "Emotionally Disturbed" due in part to the discrepancy between his high scores, failing grades and refusal to do the work. But even with new services in place no one could find the key to unlock any academic motivation.

People outside the school system love to demand that kids not be "passed along" if they haven't acquired the necessary skills, but a day inevitably comes when it's simply no longer appropriate to keep children in a school situation they have outgrown. Mickey left us to go to middle school. The next time I heard of him, several years later, he was up on charges for molesting a four year old girl after very careful, premeditated "grooming" of her and earning her trust. It seems he had also been molested for years, in fact; information he couldn't entrust even to me. A lifetime of excruciating secrecy had stolen his innocence and corroded his mind beyond repair. He spent several years in and out of juvenile correctional facilities and special education classes, his heart gradually hardening before everyone's eyes, and will be a registered sex offender for the rest of his life – how ever long or short that may turn out to be.

So who are the "monsters" and "bullies" in our society? And are they born or made? I submit that this is an extremely complex issue, too often trivialized by media and pop psychology, and nobody wants to take responsibility for their own contribution to the problem. I expressed my exasperation with this issue in the following poem that was published in a counseling journal in 1994, and while many people agreed with the message no one had a clear solution to the problem because there *is* no easy solution.

Where Were You?

Build more prisons! Fill the jails!
Eliminate paroles and bails!
Rid the streets of evil doers –
Check the alleys and the sewers!

But where were you when he was two,
With sparkling eyes and heart so true
Yet solely at the mercy of
The ones who had no time for love?

Lock the doors and windows tight;
Condemn the ones who kill and fight.
Crank up the electric chair –
The worthless scourge is everywhere.

But where were you when she was five
And happy just to be alive?
The world was such a scary place,
Already aging her sweet face.

Allocate some money, now,
And bother not with "why" or "how."
Just punish and remove them quickly –
They're irrelevant and sickly.

But where was all your passion when
Their hearts were hardening at ten;
And those of us who try, and care,
Cried out to find you were not there?

We watch their spirits flicker out
And send them on with hope, and doubt…
We mourn their sad, ironic fate –
You waited till it was too late.

There are as many explanations for cruel, heinous and twisted behaviors as there are people who manifest them; but there are also many proactive and conscious efforts toward prevention that can and should be happening all the time yet are not. While some people may actually suffer from a chemical imbalance or rare, genetic predisposition toward antisocial behaviors, it is much more often the case that negative and unhealthy experiences and influences steer people down the dark and crooked alleys of life from very early on, as depicted in another case:

A second grade boy often requested visits with me because he was fascinated with the colorful desktop computer in my room. He was a bright, beautiful child with wide, luminescent blue eyes and carefully combed brown hair. He knew how to navigate to all kinds of games and kids' websites that I didn't even know about, and when he was comfortably distracted by his own activity he would begin to talk about things going on at home. He would talk about his father beating his stepmother and his siblings and throwing people around the house; he would talk about blood, and screams, and injuries and cursing; sexual perversions, alcohol abuse, property damage and violence that he witnessed. All the while, his eyes were on the computer screen and his voice would have no particular inflection or evidence of emotion. One time I asked, "What are *you* doing when these things are going on?" Without even a shift in position, he simply stated, "Just watching." I often wonder where he is today, just as I wonder about countless other children for whom I prayed and advocated and the thousands of others whose lives come and go like anonymous wildflowers in a forgotten field.

In Virginia, according to figures that came out in 2013, a child dies from abuse or neglect every 10 days. That adds up to about 36 kids per year, in Virginia alone. The entire country and, indeed, much of the world grieved at the senseless loss of 20 precious first graders' lives during the Sandy Hook shootings in December, 2012. Why does the horror only become visceral for us when it happens in groups? How are we able to ignore the equivalent of two classrooms full of children dying needlessly every year in one state? On an even broader scale, in 2011 the national figure for deaths from child abuse and neglect were 5 per day, or 1,825 per year – approximately 91 *classrooms* full of children! Many of these deaths were very probably preventable. Until we stop compartmentalizing ourselves and our loved ones and begin to demand responsible, collaborative effort among our lawmakers and "helping" agencies, the emotionally disconnected among us will continue to wreak havoc. If *anyone* is at risk then *everyone* is at risk.

Whenever budget cuts become necessary the first things to

go always seem to be education and human services: mental health services, social services, academic enrichment services and law enforcement personnel, along with competent educators who live in the trenches and have their fingers on the pulse of the school environment every day. Cuts to administration are rare and money seems to flow readily for court services and places of incarceration for those whose inner turmoil finally explodes into the destruction of self or others.

At one point in my counseling career a group of us from the Virginia School Counselor Association had to lobby the General Assembly of Virginia for a law that would mandate professional K-12 counseling services in the schools. It had become politically trendy to demonize elementary school counselors as either unnecessary or even "dangerous" to all those allegedly perfect, intact families in which children grow. I would have been happy to be out of a job because all children had such families. Counselors at the elementary school level were reduced to the status of "optional" by a misguided governor and Board of Education. Elementary school principals were told they must choose between a counselor or a reading specialist – an illogical and unacceptable choice. These state leaders did not wish to hear that our primary source of referrals was the families themselves, overwhelmed with the responsibilities of providing basic food and shelter, or fighting the influences of the streets or the media or the entertainment industry upon their children, or struggling with domestic issues that prevented them from adequately attending to their kids. The facts just didn't fit their narrative. This was before the days of the insidious, creeping cancer of cyber bullying via social networking, so today the pressures are worse than ever. Thanks to several years of concentrated effort along with a dedicated, bi-partisan group of legislators (and a new governor) who finally grasped the bigger picture, the law was passed and continuity of care and service was restored.

Speaking of bullying, when confronted with that situation as a counselor even my own approach varied with the circumstances. Some students were clearly lashing out from a deep, aching, black hole of pain that they could not begin to put into words. Those children were actually the most reachable; they could still *feel*. Throughout history and in every culture there have been incredible heroes and leaders who overcame similar dark periods of unimaginable odds in their lives and became saints and role models for the rest of us.

Some students, on the other hand, were simply mean-spirited and apparently devoid of empathy. I didn't know until many years later that there was actually a name for this type of personality – sociopathic. These are the chameleon people who are able to adapt themselves to any environment that suits their purpose; who always have a compelling story about why they do what they do, who see no clear lines of delineation between truth and untruth and who are exaggeratedly horrified if their intentions are questioned. Many compassionate souls have experienced total depletion of time, energy and spirit trying to connect with some semblance of a heart in these people, only to repeatedly feel guilty and ashamed for doubting their motives. The good news is that sociopathic personality types are usually charming and agreeable as long as things are going their way. The bad news is that nobody really knows why they are so unreachable, or how to successfully intervene when their darker sides take over.

And then there are young people who simply have not had the qualities of good character modeled or instilled and they mimic what they see within the entertainment industry since their primary babysitters are television, internet, music, high-tech games and anything else that will keep them out of their parents' hair. Incidentally, bullying personality types come in all shapes and sizes, all ages, races, cultural and socio-economic backgrounds.

Many years ago when flipping channels on the television I found it ironic that on one station there was a huge fundraiser going on for AIDS research with dozens of famous bands, comedians, athletes and entertainers from many venues steadily bashing and blaming the government for the lack of a cure, while on most other channels these same folks were involved in show-after-prime-time-show depicting the graphic and gratuitous sex, violence and substance abuse behaviors that *cause* AIDS – without consequence. Also, these over-paid, over-valued celebrities too often play leading characters who model insulting, sarcastic humor; demeaning treatment of people who are different from them and even "humorous" verbal and physical desecration of dead bodies as if they were never human beings who lived and loved.

Our military experts discovered years ago that fighter pilots could be very successfully trained in virtual flight modules where the experience so accurately mirrored reality that they could be desensitized, in effect, and eventually programmed to transition right into the "real thing." I've always wondered why so few people connect those dots to the effects of violent, pornographic video games on children's brains; why it's the "First Amendment Right" of these game producers to desensitize our children's brains with games that reward theft, rape, murder, robbery, and all kinds of other heinous acts. People say, "Oh, they know it's just a game." My questions are, first, why is that kind of imagery acceptable as a "game" and, second, *do* they know? Is the subconscious realm of the brain really able to differentiate between what is real and what is a game or is there a desensitization and programming process occurring just as in the virtual training of pilots? How many mass shootings must occur before we ask ourselves what part we played in the overall scheme of things either through our direct involvement with the production of such negative influences or in our tolerance of them? Why are we able to conjure up vehement and self-righteous indignation at sexually pornographic images but not atrocious violence? Is that not a form of pornography as well? So who, indeed, are the monsters, the bullies and the victims? We are all guilty at some level.

When asked (often) how I could "prove" that elementary school counselors were doing anything productive I always asked in response, "How can I prove that I prevented you from being shot in the face in a parking lot?" How can anyone prove that proactive, preventive efforts work? One way we know is from the feedback of people whose lives were turned around by some caring individual who intervened at a critical time.

A constant rant about a local school jurisdiction has been its high suspension rates. Recently, buried in the metro section of the newspaper and continuing in the depths of a distant page, a report revealed that 1.78% of the students in that locality accounted for 49.4% of the suspensions. They were simply repeat offenders. And if any other determined readers took time to read the entire article they would have discovered one sentence that embodied the solution: "Far and away, the most common factor reported by those whose behavior improved was a caring adult in their lives..." The last sentence of the article, however, concluded that "...a program involving conflict resolution might be called for." I suppose the next step will be to form a committee to discuss the development of that program.

Sadly, our media choose to call our attention to the far-from-perfect side of humanity and downplay the evidence of our own divinity as much as possible. If for no other reason, money should be funneled into the proactive realm because it cannot possibly make things any worse. It has always been peculiar to me that the very people who choose careers that help their fellow man are invariably the lowest paid, least appreciated and first to be laid off in a pinch. And while I do not think that the Bible was intended to be interpreted literally, I do take the following passage very seriously:

Whoever makes himself lowly, becoming like this child, is of greatest importance in the heavenly reign. Whoever welcomes one such child for my sake welcomes me. On the other hand, it would be better for anyone who leads astray one of these little ones who believe in me, to be drowned by a millstone around his neck, in the depths of the sea. Matthew 19:4-6

The Bible isn't just a bunch of spiritual fru fru and pedagogical dogma; it's also a body of common sense advice for civil society. As a person of faith, though, I do believe that we will all be held accountable for what we did with our "gifts" while here on earth. If, for example, one has the physical, intellectual, creative and financial resources to produce movies, games or other visually entertaining products and uses those resources to damage and deflate the human spirit; or if one has a compelling gift of trustworthiness and uses it to deceive; or if one has a gift of intuitiveness and uses it to take advantage of the vulnerable among us there will be a heavy price to pay at some point in the journey of the soul.

As for the kids who are bullies and monsters within the school system specifically, sometimes we need look no further than the parents themselves who either model those behaviors or adamantly defend their children when they exhibit them. But that begs the question of which came first, the chicken or the egg? The bully or the victim?

The challenge in the public schools is that, regardless of the cause of this kind of behavior, there are no good options for school personnel who have to deal with these kids in a classroom environment. Everyone loves to tout the superiority of the private and "charter" schools – and diverse educational opportunities certainly have their merits – but rarely mentioned is the fact that these alternative institutions have the option of *removing* problematic students altogether when their behavior becomes intolerable. And where do they go? To the public schools, where no one is allowed to touch them, discipline them, suspend them, expel them, require mandatory therapy, isolate them, or anything else that would allow the other students to learn. And even if it became legally possible to temporarily or permanently remove incorrigible kids, the availability of appropriate placements or manpower to intercede is minimal to none due to tragically misplaced funding priorities both within and outside of the school system. Notice that I did not say "lack of funding" – again, money seems to flow readily for the reactive solutions.

An October 2013 headline involved a nine-year-old boy who had been suspended from school for uncontrollable behavior. The child managed to run away from home, hop on a plane and land in Las Vegas without scrutiny. When the authorities were able to locate his family, a distraught father appeared on the news pleading for help with this child. Social services had been "monitoring" the situation and the father said he and the mother had begged for help to no avail. Anyone who works in the school system was probably as un-surprised as I. Help is not available.

But getting back to the bullies – people often ask the question, why do bullies bully? There are as many reasons as there are bullies, and the cerebral study of "bullying behaviors" does nothing to address the problem. The question should be, "How do bullies continue to get away with bullying?" That's a much shorter list of answers, including but not limited to 1) they attract other bullies who want to exhibit strength in numbers, as in gangs; 2) they attract vulnerable people who live in terror of becoming their targets; and 3) – the predominant and least excusable reason – most people consider it irrelevant if it doesn't directly affect them, therefore there is no attempt to stop them. And don't think for a minute that this is a "youth problem." Bullying behaviors are pervasive at all ages, in all work environments and at all levels, all the way to government leaders and those with whom they surround themselves.

When we choose to turn our heads the other way we are as guilty as anyone wielding a threatening weapon, be it a gun, a knife, a fist, a keypad or a hateful voice.

I cut the following tiny piece out of the newspaper and held it to my heart. In summary: *July 30, 2013 – Man to serve 25 years on child porn charges… sexual battery of a minor… producing pornographic images of a minor… age 28…* I ached as I read this nondescript little blurb. The former student appeared in my mind's eye… eight years old, chubby, quiet, with a bit of a speech impediment but able to draw graphic pictures of male genitals that he referred to as "monthterth." His grandpa was in jail at the time for unspeakable crimes of molestation and the child was seeing a court-ordered psychiatrist with whom I tried to connect; even sent him the child's drawings. I multiply him in my mind to thousands of other little ones silently imploding as society turns a blind eye. *I'm so sorry, Robbie…* I sent up a prayer for him and all the others. *Father, forgive us… we know not what we do.*

What can I do?

- Pay attention! In your neighborhood, faith community, social circles – if a situation just "doesn't seem right" take time to reach out with friendship and compassion and, as suggested previously, be prepared with information about community resources.
- Don't hesitate to call the appropriate authorities if you believe a potentially dangerous situation should be investigated. If you don't know who to call, begin with the local police or sheriff's department for direction. Too many people have said, "I didn't want to get involved" only to realize later that their involvement could have saved a life.
- Start or participate in fundraisers for "safe houses" in your area. Organize a drive for supplies for these temporary homes, or assist in actually building and maintaining them.
- If you have a personal life story of beating the odds, share it! Stories of courage and inspiration serve as guiding lights out of the darkness for others.
- Stop all financial support of entertainment that glorifies bullying in any form. Violence against human dignity wears many disguises from the subtle use of sarcasm to the blatant glamorization of brutality.

Chapter 6
The Importance of Humor

Do not train children to learning by force and harshness, but direct them to it by what amuses their minds so that you may be better able to discover with accuracy the peculiar bent of the genius of each.

—Plato

Tammy, a slender, pensive third grader sat rigidly in the small chair and stared emptily at assorted materials on the child-sized table. I was on an equally small chair beside her, encouraging her to release any pent up feelings through drawing, talking, coloring, *anything*. Her words came out in a cautious staccato, her hands clasped tightly together as disturbing images projected from her lips to my giant mental movie screen. This was going nowhere; I vicariously felt the hard knot in her stomach. *Hey, God, I could use a little help here...* my most frequent prayer.

Impulsively I leapt up, clapped my hands together and theatrically exclaimed, "Oh my GOSH! I have EXACTLY what you need! You're not going to BELIEVE it! Stay right here!"

One little eyebrow slightly raised as she shifted her eyes toward my activity. I bustled over to my desk, rummaged through the bottom drawer and then excitedly headed back to the little table with both hands behind my back.

"HERE! THIS is what you need!" I proclaimed, thrusting a large bag of M&Ms in her direction.

After a startled pause Tammy exploded into laughter, causing her chair to go completely over backwards. Then we both proceeded to laugh until tears rolled down our cheeks at the sight of her feet sticking straight up into the air! We righted the chair, assessed her "injuries" and shared a little candy, then had a wonderful session of animated conversation and coloring as she poured her heart out.

The problems, as it turned out, were not insurmountable after all; just a little overwhelming and in dire need of ventilation more than anything else. And laughter was the fizz that popped the cork.

Too often, adults who work with children in distress take on an overall attitude of distress themselves. The children are defined by their problems, as in, "You know, his mother died of cancer…" or "She was sexually abused by her uncle…" or "His dad's in jail for drug dealing…" The worst thing we can do to children is forget that they are, first and foremost, *children*, and deserve opportunities to function as such. School may be the only environment for normalcy in their lives; the only place where developmentally appropriate activities can occur. And kids are FUNNY!

Even the most troubled children respond positively to the universal language of laughter. Leonard, a very bright fifth grade boy who rarely smiled, received Special Education services for both academic and behavioral concerns. Looking back with current knowledge, I wonder if he had Asperger's Syndrome. He could hack into any computer system with ease and program or de-program with the best of them. But he had tremendous difficulty with verbal or written language and his emotional development was significantly below average. When confronted with a frustrating situation Leonard tended to take on a stiff standing posture, rocking from side to side and speaking in short, clipped responses. If his issue were not progressing toward a resolution of his liking, the rocking and irritability would escalate into a full blown, irrational blowout that might include anything from name calling to profanity to physical aggression.

One of the male volunteers had made amazing inroads with him and Leonard always knew the exact days and times of his commitment to the school. He would hold himself together as well as possible in anticipation of these visits, but sometimes the inner turmoil just took over. On one such day I was called to the cafeteria where Leonard had totally lost control, jumped up and screamed threateningly at the adult and other students and, in the process, splattered himself head-to-toe with applesauce. I approached him calmly and began to escort him across the hall to my room as the cafeteria monitors angrily shouted, "Talk to him about the Code of Conduct! Call his parents! Make sure he gets suspended!" I nodded dutifully and breathed a sigh of relief as we closed my office door behind us and stood there in the quiet sanctuary for a moment, Leonard rocking back and forth and breathing heavily, fists clenched.

Finally I asked, "What happened?" Leonard began to pour out a litany of perceived injustices by the other students and, as he spoke, I kept finding myself distracted by the sparkling islands of applesauce in his course, black hair, on his skin, on his clothing, even on his glasses. I began to snicker. Leonard kept railing against his peers and my snickers rolled into an irrepressible giggle. As much as I feared that my response might exacerbate his rage, I simply could not stop myself. He finally shouted, "WHY ARE YOU LAUGHING AT ME?" Through what had now developed into grenade-like guffaws on my part, I guided Leonard to the full length mirror and squeaked out, "Look at yourself, Leonard. You are COVERED with APPLESAUCE! PLEASE tell me how that helped solve the problem in the cafeteria!"

He looked intently into the mirror for a few moments, brows furrowed, teeth gritted, and ever-so-slowly his facial muscles began to morph into a broad grin as some primal, ear-splitting semblance of laughter pierced the heaviness of the moment and ricocheted off the walls! We laughed so hard and loud that Doris poked her head in to see if everything was all right. Inevitably she, too, began to convulse with laughter at the sight of us standing there in front of that mirror, little blobs of applesauce on Leonard as well as the floor, Leonard enjoying a momentary breakthrough in self-awareness. Of course, the appropriate disciplinary measure was taken so that the child would not think his transgression could go unaddressed; but I am happy to report that his parents were supportive and he took it in stride.

Just recounting these two stories makes me laugh out loud, instantly bursting open the "laugh door" in my mind to dozens – maybe hundreds – of other comical school-related episodes involving students, faculty, parents and others whose lives zigzagged in and out of one another's in funny and joyful ways. The healing benefits of laughter were known thousands of years ago, even before this famous verse: *"A merry heart doeth good like a medicine, but a broken spirit drieth the bones"* (Proverbs 17:22). There is so much literature on the benefits of laughter that it would be impossible to cite the best sources. From basic mood enhancement to its curative powers over disease, laughter as "medicine" has been studied, observed, experienced and documented for centuries until there is very little disagreement regarding the value and, in fact, the essential need for it in our lives. So why is everybody so darn serious?

A school full of children should have an almost magical, energetic feeling. Learning should be as fun and interesting as a scavenger hunt or a hike in the woods on a crisp, autumn morning. There should be sounds of laughter and purposeful activity, music, recitation, and happy cheers for the little milestones that are reached every day. Developmentally speaking, small children do not learn from memorization but from meaningful play and tactile interaction in a respectful and clearly structured environment. Obviously, as stated earlier, there is some subject matter that can only be learned through memorization. But if most adults think back to the teachers who most inspired they will usually cite the ones who had clear boundaries along with a natural, positive "presence" and a great sense of humor. These same teachers also knew how to establish a safe place for creative and critical expression on many topics.

One of my favorite things about being in the counselor's position was the opportunity to visit classrooms and facilitate general, age-appropriate lessons that usually revolved around character development – respect, responsibility, honesty, integrity, etc. It is much more productive to talk about "character building" than "anti-bullying" with stories and imagery to which the kids can *aspire* rather than focusing on behaviors we want them to avoid. It was always interesting to walk into a classroom and "feel" the environment. Leadership, for better or worse, sets the tone in any organization; and year after year, regardless of the class mix, it seemed that the personality type at the front of the room always generated the same results. Positive, happy teachers who loved teaching almost always had positive, happy students who loved learning. Teachers who were disorganized or unprepared, ambivalent about their jobs or unclear about their role as "alpha dog" had the kids who were disorganized and often disrespectful. And teachers who were contemptuous and controlling had kids who were unmotivated, unhappy and often unwell. This is a huge simplification, of course, and doesn't take into account the challenge of truly disturbed, disruptive students whose negative patterns are ingrained before they ever enter school; but it is an accurate picture in general. Love, respect and good-humored laughter are appreciated and restorative at any age.

The art teacher at Glenside provides a great illustration – pun intended. An internationally recognized airbrush artist, Kevin's true love was teaching art to elementary school students. He was quirky, creative, irreverent and hilarious and the students loved going to his class. Sometimes, when their finished products appeared at county art exhibits, other teachers sniffed skeptically and questioned whether the students had actually done the work; but we could all vouch for them! Kevin developed a program for Glenside that he referred to as "Special Art" for fourth and fifth graders who showed precocious art ability. The catch was that they had to keep their other grades up and stay out of trouble, and this requirement usually manifested as dramatic improvement in academics, behavior and self-confidence. Occasionally he stretched his "ability prerequisites" for the sort-of-talented student who would absolutely benefit from this program, and our quiet collaborations invariably paid off. The halls were always filled with amazing creations attached to the walls, dangling from the ceilings, sitting in the corners – and many of those students went on to become recognized artists as they continued through school. Of course, there were always a few teachers who withheld the privilege as punishment for any minor transgression, totally missing the bigger picture of the benefits to everyone involved. And of course, eventually, the program was stopped because it pulled kids out of the regular classroom when they needed to be drilling for those hallowed SOLs. But the children who were lucky enough to experience those years of laughter, inventiveness, self-discipline and imagination are most likely some of our more productive members of society today.

Another hero that will always live in my heart was the school custodian, Jonas. An ex-military man, devoted husband and father, Jonas quietly kept things humming and working; clean and organized. He held the keys to the kingdom and his dry sense of humor and twinkling eyes were legendary. He could elicit trembles or giggles from kids and faculty alike with a well-placed word or look. Since so many of our students didn't have a strong male role model at home, Jonas became my go-to-guy if I felt like somebody needed a little extra attention of that sort. From thinking up little jobs he needed "help" with, to taking a walk around the playground with a little one, to speaking to the occasional assembly, Jonas provided humor and common sense where it was sometimes desperately needed. There was a brief spell where some of the boys thought it was funny to urinate into the heating vent in the bathroom, producing a steamy, acrid odor that wafted out into the hallway. Woe to them when Jonas figured out who they were! They spent many an hour on their hands and knees scrubbing that room to perfection, but loving and respecting Jonas nonetheless. He didn't play favorites, and his good heart radiated out beyond the gruff facade. Jonas was an angel in disguise.

By the previously mentioned phrase "good-humored laughter" I mean the kind that includes everyone involved; where the "joke" is for and about everyone. So how do we tell the difference between laughter that heals and laughter that hurts? We can identify what kind of humor we're engaging in by simply asking ourselves if it is inclusive or exclusive; if it's laughing *with* vs. laughing *at* someone. Children learn what they live, and if it is acceptable at home, at school or within their social network to make fun of people then they embark upon a slippery slope that often leads to bullying behaviors for a lifetime.

In my observation, anyone who says they've never been pulled into disrespectful humor is either a little self-delusional or actively lying. It usually occurs when we feel frustrated, insecure or powerless over a situation and need to build ourselves up; but that kind of "power" is like the drug that requires higher and higher doses as the good feelings wear off. When I first became a school counselor I thought certain teachers and staff were unfriendly because they didn't spend much time in the teachers' lounge or get involved in "school talk." Over time

I realized that it was more of a self-preservation tactic; they had simply learned to keep their distance from energy or conversation that might turn negative and darken their own day, ultimately affecting the children. Those were the folks who turned out to be the treasures whenever there was need for compassionate, unconditional support and the uplifting, healing kind of humor. Their names and faces remain crystal clear in my heart and mind to this day while the ones who exuded shallow, mean-spirited energy have simply become an irrelevant, conglomerate blob in my mind's eye.

Again, leadership sets the tone, and faculty members are as profoundly affected by their administrators as the children are by *them*. And school administrators are equally impacted by their jurisdictional leaders, and on it goes like an old slapstick episode of the Three Stooges – one slap begets another and another. Conversely, stories abound of people surviving the most abominable circumstances by maintaining and sharing a sense of humor; a shift in perspective that loosens the lid on the pressure cooker.

As different as we all are, we are connected by the basic commonalities of the human condition. I have always been fascinated by the diverse ways we seek to validate that connection – the bumper stickers on our vehicles, the flags on our houses, the team paraphernalia, the letters to the local paper, the tattoos, the gang graffiti… This kind of communication can be subtle or blatant, but in every instance we are saying, "This is who I am – who are you? Are you like me?" We are not so different from meerkats with their deeply embedded "pack" instinct; with the recognition of the "me/not me" as we scan the horizon for danger or safety. But sadly, also like meerkats, we seem to believe that we must always be on the lookout for those "rival mobs" that intend to do us harm. The human capacity for a healthy, objective sense of humor is really the only degree of separation between ourselves and the animal kingdom, and where it is lacking, so is civility.

Even small children recognize themselves in funny stories about children; they delight in funny jokes, funny music, funny art. And even adults – perhaps *especially* adults – require a little goofiness in their lives. In embracing our absurdities we discover our connections. A great educator knows how to be simultaneously silly and strong, compassionate and resolute, flexible and firm. In fact, the principal for whom I had the most respect during my career defined this perfect balancing act in three words: "*firm, friendly* and *fair*" – which he was. It is possible. I've seen it done with consistently positive results.

After such thoughtful introspection I cannot end a chapter on humor without telling one more story. Willard and his sister arrived at our school in the late fall, having moved in with their grandmother after the brutal stabbing death of their mother. Their father was in prison and they fantasized about living with him once he served his time for crimes unknown to us. Willard was not older than his fellow second-graders but he was way too large for the little desk and stood out in other ways as well – he was tall, overweight, verbally expressive and absolutely authentic. His emotions knew no bounds and the laughter, tears, anger, and angst flowed readily at every turn. Behind in every subject, he was fortunately assigned to a teacher who stands out in my mind as the mold from which all others should be cut. Willard was ready for third grade by the end of the year.

Throughout his time with us he endured unimaginable losses and temptations that few could survive, always maintaining an uninhibited sense of humor that threw us off guard and altered our outlook on life. One day in August, when some of us were already getting our rooms and plans in place, I was walking down a deserted hallway when I heard Willard's voice streaming in a steady monotone through a classroom door. Now in the fifth grade, he had become very close to Doris and was helping her with organizational tasks. They hadn't been in touch over the summer and I assumed they were filling in the gaps. He would speak for a few minutes and then she would quietly ask a question or offer a response; then he would speak for a few more minutes and she would respond. I strained to hear, wondering if this were something that might require another shoulder for him to lean on. I heard bits and pieces about people who had died; people who had lost babies, or moved away, or betrayed someone who trusted them; people who had caused or borne tremendous pain. I finally stuck my head in and somberly asked, "Is everything ok?" The two of them looked at each other and then erupted into laughter that reverberated throughout the room and corridor! Noting my puzzled expression, Doris finally choked out, "Oh, we're FINE! He's just catching me up on my soaps!" You just never know. Incidentally, Doris and Willard have remained friends to this day.

What can I do?

- Begin by lightening up *yourself*. Take time every day to read or watch something that makes you laugh. A gloomy, negative attitude does not empower you or anyone else.
- Treat children as children, regardless of their circumstances. The Plato quote at the beginning of this chapter carries timeless wisdom.
- If you are volunteering with kids of any age, leave your issues at the door. Equip yourself with some good (age appropriate) jokes, riddles, tricks or surprises that will pull them out of their shells and allow them to take themselves less seriously.
- Be a role model for your peers by refusing to participate

in mean-spirited humor. Others will gratefully follow your lead.

- Embrace your imperfections, admit your mistakes, laugh at yourself and create a safe environment for others to do the same. Laughing *with* rather than *at* one another is how healing begins. Reflect upon the wise lyrics of this beloved song: *Let there be peace on earth, and let it begin with me...* (Jill Jackson Miller, Sy Miller, 1955)

Chapter 7
"Good" and "Bad" Schools and Teachers

Good teachers cost a lot, but poor teachers cost a lot more.

—Evan Esar

When it comes to the issue of quality education, few topics elicit as much passion and ire as "good" and "bad" or "failing" schools and teachers. To most people, the root causes of school failure and the most effective solutions are as simple as a list of pros and cons; as two-dimensional as pictures and numbers on paper. Good. Bad. Successful. Failing. The characteristics of each are so obvious that one might wonder why any discussion is necessary at all. Unfortunately, the people with all the answers are rarely parents or school personnel whose lives revolve around centers of education, the latter of whom are under an unspoken gag order to keep their opinions to themselves.

The bad news is that there are, indeed, failing schools and teachers; in fact, there are schools that resemble war zones rather than sanctuaries of learning. There are teachers who literally live in fear for their own safety and students who would be better off with no education at all than venturing into some of these frightening establishments.

One hot, July day I had the rare luxury of dipping and floating in the ocean, releasing all cares, feeling nothing but gratitude for this perfect moment. A middle-aged woman floated on a raft nearby and we struck up one of those lazy, beach day conversations... "...beautiful day for some time at the beach"... "Where ya from?"... "I have some bottled water in my bag if you'd like some." Eventually we strolled up to our towels and, somehow, the conversation turned toward education and the impending school term. She had been out of the system for several years and was applying for positions in private schools. She loved teaching and her specialty was middle and high school science; coaching was also a passion. I was surprised that she had trouble finding work with all the emphasis on "STEM" – science, technology, engineering and math.

As the topic unfolded she hesitantly revealed that she had actually been injured on her last job in an urban school by a student who simply walked into the classroom and kicked her in the back so hard that she could barely stand. Another teacher witnessed it, and several students timidly tried to help but were met with threatening posturing by the perpetrator and his associates. The students who supported her and had a desire to learn were once again relegated to silent submission. When she reported the incident to the principal it stopped within those walls; no one would come forward as a witness, and no principal wants something like that to go on record. Her back injury forced her to take a leave of absence and, when she was ready to return to the system, "amazingly" there were no openings. Nobody wants to hire a troublemaker.

This scenario is happening all over the country as outsiders blame and complain and demand that all students remain in school under any and all circumstances. Everyone knows that the "good" teachers have perfect control of their charges, teach their subject matter flawlessly and prepare every student for higher education. Whenever I hear a news story about a teacher assaulting a student I cannot help but ponder the missing details.

The fact is, there are thousands of dedicated, tenacious teachers of every age and ethnic background who choose to work with disadvantaged populations along with those who are only there because they would never be hired anywhere else. Parents who feel powerless tend not to speak up against unacceptable situations and, in fact, are often oblivious to what goes on in their children's classrooms day after day. And students who feel isolated, inadequate, insecure and unsafe contribute to a bubbling cauldron of frustration, hopelessness and anger. Throw in decaying buildings within miles or even blocks of those "Taj Mahal" kinds of schools, outdated and insufficient books and technology, embarrassingly old team uniforms (if they have teams), aging equipment and public humiliation about test scores and there forms a perfect storm – a tsunami of negative energy to drown out any flickering embers of human dignity or hope for success.

There are also educational "leaders" who have neither the best interest of the students nor, for that matter, the best interest of the country at heart; who develop subversive political material, call it a "curriculum" and then slip it under the classroom doors across the nation while no one is paying attention. Add the short-sighted and skewed belief that every young person should go to college; that the teaching of life skills, good character and work ethics is irrelevant and a waste of time, and even a casual observer begins to wonder whose future is actually the focus. The good news is that there really are solutions; proven tactics, programs – miraculous turnarounds, in some cases – but they don't happen overnight or with a few extra dollars in the pot. They definitely don't happen in the short time span between political elections, which is a significant part of the problem, and they don't happen if the citizenry is mute and complacent.

A friend of mine was in the construction business for many years. He often bemoaned the fact that clients would become very impatient and irritated if they didn't see anything "happening" on their particular project. While he and his colleagues were surveying, measuring, developing blueprints and inventories; estimating costs, preparing a foundation, laying the groundwork; hiring and scheduling a variety of subcontractors, dealing with unpredictable weather conditions and constantly confirming that everyone involved had the same vision of the finished product, the homeowners would be literally crossing their arms, tapping their feet and scowling because nothing was getting "done." Eventually the day would come when a row of bricks would begin to take shape, or a window frame would be set, and the client would inevitably exclaim, "They're finally DOING something!" My friend referred to this as a "show day." Client and crew alike would breathe a sigh of relief, albeit for different reasons.

When politicians, media, union bosses and other outside observers of the school system begin to call the shots on education they raise the expectations of the public to ridiculous heights with pie-in-the-sky promises and well-hidden agendas. But electoral terms are relatively brief and everyone wants that "show day" as soon as the ballots are counted. Somehow, when it doesn't happen, the blame is placed upon the schools themselves rather than those who perpetuated the myths. School staff – the "crew" – may be killing themselves to try and meet the unrealistic demands and implement the often faulty plans. To use a different metaphor, a mammoth ship that has been heading in the wrong direction for years or even decades cannot suddenly reverse course. And too often, by the time it begins its gradual, creaking turn, the offshore admirals have been replaced several times and plans have changed again and again.

In the early 1980s, before I became a school counselor, I was a full time mom who found strength in numbers through the PTA. Virginia is a "Right to Work" state meaning that, while unions are legal, membership cannot be coerced. Also, the Code of Virginia states that public employees may not engage in collective bargaining – a rule I happen to agree with. In other states union members are allowed (and sometimes forced) to shut down their school systems and other government funded services through massive, endless strikes that ultimately hurt the children. Because of my lack of experience with that phenomenon I will leave the topic of union control to someone else. In Virginia we are forced to actually work out solutions through communication and collaboration, which can be both good and bad; efficient in the long run yet often tedious and exasperating in the process. More about that later.

The PTA was – and probably still is – an ideal forum for parents, school boards, school administrators and local citizens to dialogue about educational issues. Even schools not affiliated with the PTA per se can form their own home-and-school organizations for the same purpose and, as long as the relationship is civil, and as long as everyone truly has the children's highest good at heart, great things can and do happen even when the topic at hand is complex.

I recall one open meeting when I did not endear myself to the superintendent or central office leaders who were present. They had come to patiently explain to us the reasoning behind their plan to cut funding for a reading and math enrichment program since the schools in the more affluent end of the county didn't seem to need it. They simply wanted to streamline the programs across the county, claiming that there was no disparity between east and west and this would keep things "fair."

When my turn came to speak I began to tell the story of Rumpelstiltskin where, under threat of death by a greedy king, a poor miller's daughter was required to spin an entire room full of straw into gold. Rumpelstiltskin came along and performed the magical task in return for a humble piece of jewelry. Upon seeing the abundance of gold, the wicked king moved the young lady to larger and larger rooms full of straw and each time the funny little man appeared, meeting the demand for gold until the despairing girl had nothing left to give except the promise of her firstborn child. The girl's life was spared and she went on to marry and give birth to a child, at which time Rumpelstiltskin showed up to collect his due. A deal was struck whereupon she could keep the child if she could guess the man's name which, as everyone knows, she did; and the story had a happily-ever-after ending.

The point of *my* story was that teachers, too, are regularly called upon to do the impossible under threat of reprimand and even termination. Sometimes they find themselves compromising their own values to meet the demands which, as in the story, tend to grow larger and more multi-faceted with each accomplishment. In that meeting I pointed out that our talented teachers and students were every bit as eager to be successful as their more privileged neighbors to the west, but without the appropriate resources it really would be impossible. And further, each school required tools unique to its population and needs. We, the parents, suggested that if there were schools that wanted to eliminate the enrichment program then so be it, but also allow the ones who did need it to keep it.

Streamlining programs throughout our county just seemed downright silly to us. It would be like telling that crew of general contractors, subcontractors and construction workers to get started on the job and then handing each of them a hammer. And yet, what's trending today is streamlining a controversial curriculum throughout the entire *nation*! While basic academic skill development does have some universal essentials, there are many paths to the same destination which, ideally, is preparation for *life*. My mother-in-law was an outstanding and highly respected elementary school teacher during the early to mid 1960s. We have had many conversations about effective educational visions and tactics over the years, but one comment of hers has always stuck with me. She said, "Certain kids are never going to be able to read perfectly, or excel in math or become academic superstars. If my principal had come to me and threatened to shoot me if everyone wasn't on grade level by the end of the year I would have told him to go ahead and shoot now."

At the end of my little presentation to the local school leaders, the superintendent was clearly annoyed but maintained his composure when the other parents applauded. To the county's credit, we did keep that enrichment program and felt empowered to remain *vigilant* and *vocal* as other issues arose. As simplistic as this sounds, this is a major key to "fixing" the public school system – community members must be vigilant and vocal every step of the way. And again, like it or not, the "village" must take responsibility for its own. Before that can happen, though, people must feel like they are *part* of a village; they must believe that their voice, their vote, their needs, their gifts and skills make a difference not just locally but in the larger scheme of things. Those who complain that they should not have to support the public schools if they don't have children in those schools need to understand that the child they save today could be the one who saves them tomorrow; or, more bluntly, the one they don't save may be the one who guns them down in a movie theater some day when the feelings of detachment become too much to bear.

I previously mentioned that being forced to work out solutions through communication and collaboration can be both good and bad. The benefits are clear. When everyone participates in developing the plan, everyone feels invested in the outcome. The downside is that too few people are willing or motivated to become involved in the process, often leaving the largest egos to battle things out. Like any bureaucracy, the public school system has its good guys and bad guys; people who go into the field for altruistic reasons and those who simply seek positions of control wherever possible.

In lower socioeconomic areas people often feel powerless for many reasons, some legitimate and some imagined. Legitimate reasons might include work responsibilities that prevent their availability, or lack of transportation to meetings, or actual rude treatment by school officials who make them feel unwelcome or irrelevant. Perhaps they lack education themselves and are intimidated, or simply lack information regarding their legal right to have a say in the system.

In many cases, parents who live in challenging or dangerous localities have spotty or personally traumatic memories of school themselves and, thus, buy into the myth that they have nothing to contribute to the conversation. That would fall into the "imagined" category of reasons to feel powerless, along with a tendency to trust that school professionals will always know and do what is best for their children. Parents who are unaware of the power of their own rights may as well have no rights. Educational professionals at every level are employed by the people and are entrusted with the children of the people to provide the academic piece of a foundation for life. And while they are specially trained to do this, it is also incumbent upon them to empower parents with any information that might help them advocate for their children on the educational journey. When the communication and collaboration happens only among the professionals, a natural imbalance and resulting crash will most certainly occur.

Unfortunately, when parents feel powerless for *any* reason and refuse to engage in their children's education, teachers have no recourse as problems arise. Many a caring, gifted teacher has grieved for the kids whose academic and behavioral issues grew worse and worse as parents refused to return phone calls, show up for conferences, sign or return notes or offer any insight into the picture. As the public demands that schools stop suspending disruptive students, and as the legal community chomps at the bit to prosecute anyone who tries, all learning comes to a screeching halt. The truly disturbed young people know that there is neither help nor consequence for their poor choices either at home or at school and the school environment becomes an extension of their perilous neighborhoods. As parents with the means and commitment to a better education begin to move away, transport their kids to a different school or home school them, the worst of the worst will be left under one roof.

As the obsession with a standardized curriculum and standardized test scores becomes the primary measure of "good" schools, outstanding teachers often relocate or leave the profession altogether. Again, the uncomfortable truth is that, while the neediest schools often attract the most determined and dedicated educators, they are also left in the hands of many incompetent teachers and administrators who would otherwise not be hired anywhere else but who are gratefully retained by a school that desperately needs them.

People regularly say that we can't save everyone; we need to focus on those who CAN be saved. But who is qualified to make that call? Is that not the equivalent of a "death panel" of sorts? Should we not begin with a basic assumption that *all* children deserve to be saved, and then do our very, very best to provide appropriate services and interventions wherever necessary? As people begin to choose alternative methods of instruction, should society become resigned to the "fact" that some kids are simply throwaways and allow the schools in crisis to be nothing more than criminal incubators? Or should we take a look at what is actually working in schools that succeed – public, private or home – and then make every effort to reproduce those models in creative, optimistic ways? Have we become such cynical curmudgeons that the hopes and dreams of our forefathers (and foremothers) have gone by the wayside?

Where poor or nonexistent parenting is rampant, there is

no reason why a school system could not offer after school tutoring, mentoring, activities (and food, if necessary) for the children along with skill building and educational opportunities for willing parents. There was one period of time when a group of us pleaded with our central office leaders to provide after-school transportation for children who needed that kind of help. We were willing to work beyond contractual hours for no extra pay just to stay and tutor or supervise homework. I witnessed many children who were excellent students in the classroom; who earned top grades on class work and tests but did not have a home environment that supported homework time. The teachers actually averaged zeros into their grades, dropping the entire GPA to average or below average, condemning them to a school-life journey of low achieving classes and drastically reducing their chances of transitioning into higher education or even high paying jobs. They had no choice – if there were no consequences for skipping homework then it would not be long before the other students would refuse to do it. Our county absolutely would not agree to after-school transportation for elementary school students. It was too expensive. It was a frivolous idea. It was only for middle and high school students. We knew that by the time our at-risk kids reached middle and high school it would be too late; they would have fallen too far behind to catch up without extensive, focused, individualized attention which, we also knew, wouldn't happen. I will always wonder why county and city governments don't see the cost-effectiveness of proactive spending. It is far more costly to support people for years in the welfare or correctional system than to identify and nurture their gifts in the formative years.

Perhaps we could raise our collective low self esteem regarding global test score comparisons by remembering that in America we promise to educate *all* children, and therefore *all* test scores are averaged for *all* the world to see. Unlike most countries, we don't separate the intellectual cream of the crop from everyone else in elementary school and then track them onto a path toward higher education, leaving the other students' scores out of the mix. I imagine that the comparisons might be quite different if only the scores of our academically gifted students were depicted in those graphs. It might present a more level and pleasing visual of the playing field, but it would also fly in the face of everything we Americans purport to believe about the importance of educating everyone.

A "good" or "bad" school or teacher can be any place. Success and failure, depending on how you define them, cross all socioeconomic lines. Whenever I hear about an "Educational Summit" I always dig into the information to see how many parents, counselors, teachers and school administrators have a seat at the table. Usually there are few or none. There always seems to be an abundance of money available for the things our leaders consider important. In 2013 Virginia endured a seemingly endless gubernatorial race where the candidates spent approximately fifty-five *million* dollars – that's $55,000,000 – on sarcasm, deceit, embellishments and lies. As their printed, televised and cyber-ads invaded my personal and professional space at every turn, all I could think about was how much good all that money could have done for our Commonwealth; all I could see was the faces of children scrolling across my mind with their trusting, hopeful eyes. They are totally at our mercy.

The central problem of failing schools is not a lack of funding but, rather, a pervasive inability or refusal of leaders at every level to truly grasp the bigger picture and then forge ahead with well-laid, long term plans. It's about territorial attitudes, short-sighted goals, bloated egos and skewed priorities. Sadly, it's about putting the highest good of our children last.

What can I do?

- If you have ever been employed by a school system, you have a wealth of knowledge and experience to impart about how the system operates. Become a parent advocate. Join an established home-school organization where you can share your expertise, or start an informal parent support group yourself.
- The biggest obstacle to after-school assistance at the elementary level is transportation. If you are willing to submit to a background check and obtain a CDL (Commercial Driver's License) you may be allowed to offer this desperately needed service.
- Find out if any of the local day care centers allow volunteers to come in and tutor or help children with homework and then sign up!
- Show appreciation for school faculty! A thoughtful letter to the local paper, a little treat during Teacher Appreciation Week or a simple "Thank you for all you do" when you encounter a professional educator outside of school goes a very long way. Any form of positive reinforcement means more to them than you will ever know.
- School personnel actually do exist under a gag order when it comes to expressing concerns about their situations. If you are aware of circumstances that are unsafe or unacceptable, be the voice!

Chapter 8
Hidden Treasures

Be not forgetful to entertain strangers: for thereby some have entertained angels unawares..."

—Hebrews 13:2

Mrs. Stafford had her hands full. She was definitely not the envy of her co-workers who gratefully sent their rambunctious, learning disabled third graders to her classroom every day for reading and math. Some students were in her class all day, "self-contained" as the lingo goes, and for some she was "resource." In any case, these were children who had an average to high IQ but simply could not seem to learn successfully in the traditional classroom environment. They had been through all the steps to determine their "eligibility" for these special services. These were some of the dreaded Special Needs Kids who cause school administrators' hair to turn prematurely gray, who cost the county a bundle of money and whose rights are actually protected by the federal government.

But before I continue with a story about this particular class, allow me to provide a little history of Special Education in the United States. While Special Education sometimes goes by different names (such as "Exceptional Education") in different localities and while children are under the legal guardianship of a variety of adults with different titles, for the sake of brevity I will use the terms "Special Education" and "parents" to refer to these. Volumes have been written on this subject. Numerous laws, multiple acts of Congress and hundreds of amendments have modified and fine-tuned the regulations and definitions surrounding the terms "handicapped" and "disabled" over the past hundred years. The following summary is intended to highlight the most significant steps that led to current practices of educating students with special needs within the public school system.

Like most humane programs that begin with the best of intentions, this vision began as a grassroots advocacy effort of parents in the early 20th century. One can only imagine the dichotomy of powerful forces in place at that time with this group passionately humanizing the physically, emotionally and intellectually challenged while a much larger and more vocal group was simultaneously pushing for selective breeding or "eugenics" in several countries including the United States. Some of our most revered leaders – including Margaret Sanger, Presidents Theodore Roosevelt and Woodrow Wilson to name a few – were part of the early Progressives who firmly believed in the gradual annihilation of the "feebleminded" (as well as those considered racially inferior to themselves) through involuntary sterilization and birth control. Sanger, in her book *The Pivot of Civilization* (published in 1922) summed it up this way:

> "...it should always be remembered that feeble-mindedness is not an unrelated expression of modern civilization. Its roots strike deep into the social fabric. Modern studies indicate that insanity, epilepsy, criminality, prostitution, pauperism, and mental defect, are all organically bound up together and that the least intelligent and the thoroughly degenerate classes in every community are the most prolific. Feeble-mindedness

in one generation becomes pauperism or insanity in the next. There is every indication that feeble-mindedness in its protean forms is on the increase, that it has leaped the barriers, and that there is truly, as some of the scientific eugenists have pointed out, a feeble-minded peril to future generations – unless the feeble-minded are prevented from reproducing their kind. To meet this emergency is the immediate and peremptory duty of every State and of all communities."

Oh, to have been a fly on the wall and heard first-hand the vitriol that must have been lobbed back and forth between these groups!

While even Thomas Jefferson had strongly and often recommended the education of "the whole mass of the people", parents of children with special needs at the peak of the eugenics movement had few options other than home schooling, expensive private education or, frankly, neglect. After decades of what surely must have been tenacious determination, the will of the people began to manifest in 1961 when President John F. Kennedy created the "President's Panel on Mental Retardation" which eventually resulted in federal aid to the states. President Lyndon B. Johnson expanded upon this when he signed the "Elementary and Secondary Education Act" in 1965.

In spite of these efforts, few children with disabilities of any sort were being educated in the public schools. In 1970, Congress passed the "Early Education for Handicapped Children" program – the government's first tangible move in the direction of early academic intervention for the disabled. The "Rehabilitation Act" of 1973 (Public Law 93-112) prohibited discrimination, based on disability, within any federally funded programs or businesses and laid the groundwork for Title I of the American Disabilities Act of 1990. In 1975 Congress passed "The Education for All Handicapped Children Act"

(EHA – Public Law 94-142) requiring all states to provide a "Free, appropriate public education" to school-age children with handicaps in "the least restrictive environment." In October of 1990, Congress passed the "Individuals with Disabilities Education Act" (IDEA – Public Law 101-476), which reauthorized parts of the EHA and added and changed some of the definitions and related services for disabled school children.

While the language around this subject continues to evolve, and though amendments have been added, deleted and tweaked over time, the IDEA was the law that unequivocally acknowledged the *right* to a public education for all children and required specifically tailored academic plans to meet the individual needs of disabled children in government funded public schools. That academic plan is known as an "Individualized Education Program" or IEP and must not only basically benefit the child but also provide appropriate preparation for the future. It also mandates that the school must take the child's disability into consideration whenever disciplinary action might be necessary.

In Virginia, according to the Department of Education website, the Code reads as follows:

Code of Virginia § 22.1-214, Board to Prepare Special Education Program for Children With Disabilities.

> *The Code of Virginia requires the Board of Education to ensure that each school division in Virginia has a special education program to educate and train children with disabilities. Virginia requires that all children with disabilities between the ages of 2 and 21, inclusive (i.e., ages 2 through 21), be identified, evaluated and have made available to them a free and appropriate public education (FAPE). School divisions are mandated to comply with these regulations under Article VIII, Section*

I of the Constitution of Virginia, Title 22.1 of the Code of Virginia, and the federal Individuals with Disabilities Education Act (20 U.S.C. Section 1400-1485)

Over the years, specific labels have been developed to help the schools zero in more effectively on many different types of physical, emotional and intellectual disabilities. While the identification process is more clear-cut in the case of obvious physical and medically-founded disabilities, there exists a rather expansive "gray area" when behavioral issues are under scrutiny. Unlike the "Diagnostic and Statistical Manual of Mental Health Disorders" (DSM-5) developed by the American Psychiatric Association for mental health professionals, the terminology and definitions utilized by school professionals must include ramifications of the handicapping condition upon academic progress and success. This is significant, because if a child exhibits certifiable mental health disorders and disturbing behaviors yet maintains decent grades, then he or she will not qualify for any Special Education services. (As one school psychologist "sensitively" put it to me, "We can't do anything if they're just *crazy*.") This can be a mixed blessing. If the unacceptable behaviors are dangerous to self or others and the child has not qualified for an IEP, then disciplinary action can be taken, limited though it may be. On the other hand, if a child *with* an IEP does exactly the same things then the school must hold a series of meetings known as "causal hearings" (while the child in question continues to attend school) to determine whether the behavior was within the realm of the handicapping condition or not. If it was, then no disciplinary action (such as suspension) may be taken because, basically, the bad behavior isn't considered to be the child's fault. At this point it is left to the teacher to devise consequences that must be carried out within the classroom, which is usually where the child did not follow the rules already in place…

Practically speaking, the implementation of IDEA works like this:

– A child is suspected (sometimes as early as preschool age) of having a handicapping condition which may include anything from the following list of qualifiers: *Those children evaluated as having autism, deaf-blindness, a developmental delay, a hearing impairment (which may include deafness), mental retardation, multiple disabilities, an orthopedic impairment, other health impairment, a serious emotional disturbance, a severe and profound disability, a specific learning disability, a speech or language impairment, a traumatic brain injury, or a visual impairment (which may include blindness), who, because of these impairments, need special education and related services* (Virginia D.O.E. "School Health Guidelines"). Incidentally, each of those qualifiers is a "heading" for a sub-list of characteristics that must be explored.

– The meetings that follow have different names in different localities, but in my jurisdiction they were referred to as "Child Study Team" meetings. These initial gatherings are attended by parents, teachers, the school social worker and school psychologist (who are assigned to several hundred students in different schools), the school counselor, the principal or designee and any other mutually approved parties involved with the child under consideration. Except in the case of preschoolers who are not already enrolled, the classroom teacher must attend the meeting and leave lessons plans for a paid substitute who will cover the class. Each school has a designated "Child Study Team" day to accommodate everyone's schedules, and sometimes the referrals consume the entire day for most of the personnel involved.

– All present provide input and feedback and discuss the probable causes for concern, and a list of strategies to address the issues is generated for the teacher and the parents. Another meeting will be scheduled as follow-up, usually in no fewer than six weeks, to evaluate the effectiveness of the strategies. If, at that future meeting, the teacher reports that the problems have been resolved and the student is making progress, then the team closes the file until further notice. If, however, the problems have continued or become worse, then the team generates more strategies and schedules another follow-up.

– If, after several Child Study Team consultations, the child is showing little or no improvement then the team may approve the initiation of a "Full Evaluation" process to determine whether or not the child has a handicapping condition that qualifies for an Individualized Education Program (the IEP) within Special Education services. This process – which legally must be completed by a given deadline – includes the following reports (Virginia D.O.E.):

Assessment Components of Suspected Disability

Component Description:

- *Educational – Written report describing current educational performance and identifying instructional strengths and weaknesses in academic skills and language performance.*

- *Medical* – Written report from a licensed physician indicating general medical history and any medical/health problems that may impede learning.
- *Sociocultural* – Written report from a qualified visiting teacher or school social worker that describes family history, structure, and dynamics; developmental and health history; and social/adaptive behavior in the home, school, and community. The information is obtained through interviews with parents or primary caretakers in addition to use of other social appraisal methods.
- *Psychological* – Written report from a qualified psychologist based on the use of a battery of appropriate instruments that shall include individual intelligence test(s) and psycho-educational tests.
- *Developmental* – Written report of assessment of how the child functions in the major areas of development (such as cognition, motor, social/adaptive behavior, perceptions, and communications), where required in the regulations for assessing the specified handicapping conditions.
- *Other* – Where indicated (e.g., audiological, speech-language). All assessments must be provided in written format and must be conducted by qualified personnel. To be qualified, professionals must meet any applicable licensing requirements.

When all of the component reports have been completed by the team members, the case transitions from the Child Study Team to the Eligibility Team, which is basically the same group. Each report is thoroughly discussed, always in relation to the potential academic success of the student. Discussing and determining a handicapping condition, or label, ahead of time is illegal; the decision for or against eligibility must be made by the team at the time of this meeting. And the qualifying child's needs must never be adapted to existing programs. If available services are insufficient then the school must create a new program for the child.

If, at the conclusion of this process, the Eligibility Team cannot find irrefutable evidence of a handicapping condition that is contributing to the student's lack of success then the student, teachers and parents return to Square One – attempting to find new tactics to help the child succeed. If, however, the team agrees that the child has an identifiable handicapping condition that meets the federal and state guidelines, then the case transitions from the Eligibility Team to the IEP Team. This team will include the Special Education teacher who is most qualified and trained to address the academic needs of similarly-labeled students and who will most likely become the teacher of the child in question.

The purpose of the IEP is to clearly define – in minute, written detail – that customized program, and the plan must be completed within a designated period of time following the identification of the student. Upon completion of this document and after obtaining all of the legally required signatures, the teacher will then add this student to the roll and continue to teach his or her class within the least restrictive environment according to each IEP. If, over time, the child continues to be unsuccessful, then the Eligibility Team will reconvene and discuss a more restrictive environment (such as the self-contained option mentioned earlier) to give the child more concentrated attention; then the IEP Team will meet again to modify the written plan. Sometimes the meetings, modifications and restrictions continue until it becomes clear that the child cannot succeed in any program within the regular school, at which point he or she may be moved to a school whose entire student population is comprised of the most physically and emotionally or intellectually handicapped. And if that most-restrictive environment also proves inadequate, then the school system of residence must pay for the required "free and appropriate education" from a private institution that offers daily or even residential services. That can be extremely expensive and elaborate efforts are made to avoid this option at all costs, literally.

Left-brain pause for reflection: All of the above probably sounds like just another pile of government gobbledygook but, actually, the laws and procedures described thus far are designed to benefit those among us who truly cannot effectively advocate for themselves. Those turn-of-the-20th-century educational pioneers would surely be pleased to know that their vision of a just and moral society won out over the eugenics movement. And while the complexity of the rules and regulations protecting the disabled will always need continuous pruning and refining, hopefully most people would find them preferable to the legally sanctioned eradication of segments of our species that the early Progressives deemed unworthy to exist.

My words up to this point in the book have not been meant to demonize *all* politicians and public/private sector leaders; many people throughout history have dedicated their lives to improving the lives of others. They are the healers, the ones who will be remembered and cherished by future generations – sometimes in small numbers, sometimes globally – while the others crumble into nondescript memory dust. In 1991 I wrote the following sonnet to honor these unsung heroes:

The Healer

A weary earth renews itself once more,
As cries of anguish echo through the years.
Life springs forth from jagged scars of war
To find man still imprisoned by his fears.
But though the tools of hatred yet abound,

And conquerors proclaim the vict'ry theirs,
The power of the healer makes no sound
Yet fortifies, emboldens and repairs.
And who has most enlightened and inspired?
And who is most remembered from the past?
Destruction leaves the spirit torn and tired;
Rejuvenation builds the soul to last.
Though swords may clash and mighty towers fall,
The healer has the greatest strength of all.

Left-brain reconnect: Getting back to the actual application of IDEA within a school, of course each of the teams and committees requires an on-site chairman who must constantly coordinate everyone involved and make sure that deadlines are met, and whose job it is to be sure that all of the information is complete and always organized according to certain specifications in the child's permanent records file. There are serious legal consequences for violating the regulations. This person is a faculty member with the usual load of responsibilities connected to his or her position, so many off-contract hours are spent juggling the clerical aspects of all this and communicating with relevant family members who cannot meet or talk during the school day. At the same time, many contractual hours that should be devoted to the students are poked full of holes as school personnel participate in the various teams. Meanwhile, the ongoing business of lesson planning, grading class work and educating children in general must be squeezed in somewhere. In thinking about those who dispense ordinances and those who must apply them, an old Spanish proverb comes to mind: *It is not the same thing to talk of bulls as to be in the bullring.*

At the meetings that take place once a child has been found

eligible for services the parents are given a legal document that outlines their rights every step of the way. Someone on the team is required to review this document with them to confirm that they fully grasp the significance of their role; to be sure they understand that they are *always in control* of any decisions made regarding their child. The parents have the final say, always. Even if a child qualifies for Special Education services, the parents can decide against authorization and take their chances on continuing with the regular curriculum. Conversely, if the school's evaluation does not prove that a handicapping condition exists but the parents are convinced something was missed, they can obtain other assessments from professionals in the private sector and this new information must be taken into consideration. This is the balance of power if parents understand their rights… and this is part of that gray area.

As previously mentioned, many parents are disconnected from their children's academic journey for a variety of reasons, not the least of which is the feeling of intimidation by all those seemingly elite, degree-bearing show-offs who sit around the team table. Whether that impression is based in reality or not, the visceral effect is the same. Unfortunately there are unscrupulous people within the system who can sniff out that kind of insecurity and use it to their own advantage – sometimes with the blessing of central office department directors. The task of determining whether or not children are eligible for services is actually a rather multi-faceted dilemma at times and not as straightforward as implied in the practices outlined above. There is just enough wiggle room within those "written reports" and "individual intelligence tests" and "socio-cultural… appraisal methods" and "psycho-educational tests" for a certain amount of subjectivity that can, in fact, tip the resulting profile toward a desired outcome.

On the one hand, everyone working in the school system agrees (hopefully) that all children deserve to be successful. On the other hand, "successful" is defined as "high scoring" and knowledge is not always demonstrable via traditional tests. On still another hand, it is tempting to apply a handicapping condition to someone whose low scores might otherwise impact the overall average of the school – Special Education test scores are categorized differently because of all the modifications required by those students' IEPs. And on still another hand, it's also tempting to keep the number of eligible students as low as possible to minimize the budgetary impact on the county. There has also been negative publicity and thus, sensitivity about the over-labeling of minorities with challenging cultural backgrounds. There are many hands contributing to and stirring this pot at any given moment.

The teams that make these life-altering decisions for children always have interesting personality dynamics. If there is disagreement on what is in the best interest of the child, meetings can be very prolonged and uncomfortable; if everyone agrees then the job at hand is collaborative and pleasant. Sometimes there are hidden agendas that don't rear their ugly heads until the parents arrive, at which time all parties must decide whether it's better to engage in contentious banter or keep quiet. Meticulous notes are kept at each meeting and sometimes recorded; words must be very well considered before spoken aloud.

One school psychologist was the darling of the department for "keeping the numbers down" and actually did a lot of the training and in-service workshops for her colleagues. She was renowned for using elevated, academic rhetoric in meetings with parents who had no idea what she was talking about; heads would dutifully nod and signatures would flow across the dotted lines. Even team members could become mesmerized by her faux compassionate, intellectual explanations, only to be startled by a conclusion with which they did not agree. Sometimes the teachers and counselors who knew the children best would boldly step in as interpreters for the grateful parents and the conversation would continue until everyone felt comfortable with the decision.

Although innumerable, blatant examples are parading through my mind, I must shift gears and point out that there are also tyrannical, misinformed parents who monopolize these meetings with unrealistic and even illegal demands at times. Threats of lawsuits from either or both sides hover in the air like tanks of poison gas positioned to release at any moment with, as usual, the children hanging in the balance. Some parents insist on Special Ed services for kids who don't qualify, as this provides virtually unlimited access to faculty time and energy as well as a lifelong excuse for their own poor parenting skills (*Well, he has a handicapping condition, you know...*). Other parents whose children desperately need the expertise of the Special Education teachers refuse to allow a "label" even though the interventions are intended to be temporary if at all possible. And the precious minutes and hours of the school day tick by...

But what of Mrs. Stafford's class, the learning disabled third graders who opened this chapter? It was a relatively small and racially diverse group of boys and girls; this one with serious health issues, that one already aligning with neighborhood gangs, some chronically angry and frustrated as they struggled with feelings of personal and academic failure at every turn. Most of them absolutely qualified for the Special Education program while others probably slid in due to the aforementioned "wiggle room" of the assessors. One thing they had in common was an unabashed love for Mrs. Stafford. Her sense of humor, faith in them and tendency toward an appropriate level of self-disclosure made them feel safe, accepted and optimistic.

Mrs. Stafford had been unable to have children. She had been pregnant several times and endured several agonizing miscarriages, including at least one baby that was full term. Now she was pregnant again, beyond the "danger zone" for early loss, and the children were giddy with excitement as her belly ripened day by day. They couldn't wait until the arrival of this little one, as if it were their own brother or sister on the way. Sometime between the second and third trimester, however, the worst news happened again. Mrs. Stafford was in the hospital… the baby had been born prematurely and dead. How were we ever going to break the news to this class?

Following the *I could use a little help here* prayer, I talked to her aide about allowing me to come in and bring construction paper for the kids to make cards for Mrs. Stafford. I would break the news, with her assistance, and we would help them with their cards. These were, remember, kids with learning disabilities that affected reading, handwriting, verbal and written expression; not to mention that this was a very delicate topic to discuss with children under *any* circumstances. I would be The Comforter, The Adult. I was wrong. As usual, the children were the teachers.

Before I even finished the opening sentence they knew the news. These kids were not strangers to the pain of loss. Silence, tears, a few questions and then dogged determination to make the very best cards in the world for their beloved teacher. Plain paper was magically transformed with elaborate colors, pictures, ragged words of love and encouragement that I didn't know they knew as crayons and markers flew back and forth. Some requested correct spellings, some were not the least concerned; Mrs. Stafford would know what they meant. She read their hearts every day. With my own tears finally in check I began to collect the masterpieces and noticed a scene that I will treasure forever. Two of the "roughest" boys in the class who were not particularly good friends were huddled with desks pushed together, one quietly sobbing, his head down on his desk. The other spoke quietly in his ear, a protective arm almost encircling him. A snapshot of pure, unconditional love.

Mrs. Stafford loved her cards and returned to school after

her time of recovery. Eventually she had not just one healthy baby but two. The beauty of a little neighborhood school is that most of the families stick around, and most of these kids got to see the babies. I'm sure that no one, save Mrs. Stafford, could have possibly been more thrilled.

My soul bows in reverence to the Special Education teachers of the world, whose inimitable x-ray vision penetrates the outer trappings and sees straight to the essence of their charges. They are definitely among the healers described in my poem. Whether their students are legitimately there for handicapping conditions or not, their expertise in breaking a lesson down into bite-sized parts – allowing time to chew, swallow and digest before the next bite – is amazing and humbling to watch. They make the incomprehensible comprehensible and celebrate every "aha moment" as if it were their own. I include teachers of gifted students in this praise as well because they, too, are usually following individualized plans and tapping every creative cell in their being to meet the needs of these unique children. These are the ones who should be teaching *teachers* instead of the preponderance of stuffy professors who inhabit the sterile walls of academia. If only *all* children could benefit from this level of ingenuity and imagination! I often wonder how many students who are diagnosed with ADD and ADHD simply have different learning styles and might thrive under such tutelage.

Regrettably, within the hierarchy of school professionals, the teachers of special needs children probably receive the least amount of attention and acclaim. Their students, after all, do not generally elevate the test scores and, in fact, these special classes are often unwelcome in the hallowed halls of "regular" schools. The children are "different" from the mainstream, often lacking in self-control and, God-forbid, sometimes unsightly. But anyone who has ever become involved with the community of the "impaired" discovers a wonderful secret society of sorts where communication among both adults and children occurs with a glance, a smile, a gesture, a tear or a cheer at any given moment. They seem to cherish each new day, count the smallest of blessings and rarely sweat the small stuff. They are the hidden treasures of our society, unintentionally providing inspiration and every bit deserving of the laws that protect them.

A vivid memory from my own elementary school years comes to mind. One day the Mother Superior appeared in our classroom and began to talk about people with different kinds of disabilities. Perhaps one of my classmates was ashamed of someone at home; I will never know what prompted that visit. In any case, she wrapped up her lesson with a wide-eyed, conspiratorial expression like one might don before announcing that the Easter Bunny is coming, swept her gaze from one side of the room to the other and quietly said, "If you have a mentally retarded person in your family then you have an angel living in your house!" OH how we all wanted that! I am absolutely sure that those of us who witnessed that magical revelation have viewed the physically, emotionally or intellectually disabled with a touch of awe ever since.

What can I do?

- If you are the parent or guardian of a child with special needs:
    - First and foremost, *know your rights*. Study the information the school is required to give you. This absolutely cannot be emphasized enough.
    - Never allow school personnel to intimidate, coerce, condescend to you or rush you. Ask questions. Appropriate planning for your child's future is a team effort and you are the captain.

- If you cannot attend all of the meetings, authorize a designee who understands the process and can interact knowledgeably.
- Be considerate of the teachers' and other professionals' time. They are trying to help many students who need specialized assistance.
- Educate yourself about your child's handicapping condition as it relates to academic performance so that you can be the expert at home. Respectful collaboration between parents and teachers is a recipe for success.

- Whether or not you have a child with special needs there are many ways to make a difference in the lives of these children. Like the parents, first take time to learn about the legal and academic rights afforded to the disabled. Abundant information can be found at the federal, state and local levels with a simple internet search.
- If you have the gift of time, apply to become a teacher's aide in a special education classroom. These are paid positions and paraprofessionals are always needed.
- Volunteer with (or donate to) the Special Olympics.
- Encourage your children to befriend children with special needs – to sit with them at lunch, invite them to birthday parties, treat them like anyone else. They will become role models for their peers.

Chapter 9
The Seamy Underbelly

When you teach your son, you teach your son's son.

—The Talmud

The tattered, black gift bag was stuffed into the corner of a file cabinet drawer in my home office. What silly thing had I hoarded away this time? I dug it out, peered inside and saw the worn, stained, stuffed bunny... my mind immediately flashed back to 1999.

"Do we have enough toys for the children yet?"

"What do we still need?"

"When are you taking everything to the children?" Imploring eyes searched my own as the children asked, day after day, about the Christmas project to provide a new toy for every child in a distant school that had almost been destroyed by hurricane floodwaters in the fall. I was the SCA sponsor and every year we tried to come up with some kind of a school-wide outreach project during the Christmas season. The socioeconomic diversity of our own population made it sort of a sacred challenge for me – I have always considered outreach the ultimate cure for depression, but I didn't want to put a strain on anyone who simply could not give.

One evening there had been a news clip about the little town of Franklin, VA – about 80 miles away – that was still struggling to recover from the devastation to their homes, schools and businesses after Hurricane Floyd mercilessly swept through and nearly wiped them off the map. I asked my principal, Dr. Newsome ("firm, friendly and fair"), what he thought about our kids reaching out to their elementary school with a new toy for each child. There were some big logistical pros and cons, not the least of which was the fact that they had almost 200 more students than we did. Dr. N. was a man of faith and believed it would be a mutually beneficial endeavor. Approved.

At the next SCA meeting I presented the idea to the student reps – third, fourth and fifth graders chosen by their classmates along with officers who were elected by the whole school. Their enthusiasm was overwhelming and we set about organizing a way to bring in the gifts. After a call to the school in Franklin to make our project known and get a head count for each grade level, the SCA kids and I began cutting out color-coded, grade-level specific male and female shapes for the students to take home with a letter of explanation about the program – what the spending limit was, how to determine whether to provide a gift for a boy or a girl, what age, etc. We had a budget for the wrapping supplies and as the gifts began to come in we spread everything out on the stage, swiftly wrapping and crossing things off one by one. Noting the imbalance of our numbers to theirs, several faculty members' churches and local day care centers also sent in items of all shapes and sizes. I remember sitting on the stage alone one afternoon, surrounded by these loving contributions but wondering if we had bitten off way more than we could chew. Again the prayer, *Ummm, hey, God? I could use a little help here!* Several parents became celestial assistants over the next few weeks, showing up during and after school hours to stay on top of the growing piles and offering to be part of the eventual caravan. Kevin, the art teacher from my previous school, created a poster depicting the two schools' mascots and had it laminated. The secretary at the Franklin school informed us that their holiday didn't begin until a few days after ours, which provided a perfect window of opportunity for an agreed-upon delivery day.

The excitement grew among the students and, as Dr. N and I hoped, the positive energy surrounding the project manifested in overall improvement in attitudes and behavior. We were a team, and even the children who were accustomed to getting very little on their own Christmas mornings were filled with the spirit of the season; thus, the questions, "Is there enough? Are we ready?"

One day I headed into my office and discovered a tattered, black gift bag containing a worn, stained, stuffed bunny... I thought of the words of the Skin Horse from *The Velveteen Rabbit:* "...Generally, by the time you are Real, most of your hair has been loved off, and your eyes drop out and you get loose in the joints and very shabby. But these things don't matter at all, because once you are Real you can't be ugly, except to people who don't understand"— Margery Williams, *The Velveteen Rabbit*. My eyes teared up as I imagined the child who sacrificed this treasure for someone less fortunate, and I tucked it away with a prayer for guidance about its future... I couldn't really include it with all the new things, but I didn't want to offend the heart of the giver.

In the midst of all this, a Central Office administrator showed up one morning before the announcements just to visit the school and touch base with Dr. N. She had always been one of the "good guys" in my experience; a genuine advocate for elementary school students and faculty. I showed her the box on the office counter with extra cut outs for parents or visitors to pick up along with our letter and our "vision." I was so excited I could hardly take a breath as I explained the goal, the process and the wonderful effect on the students, staff, parents and community. She was very distracted, looking at the clock, only half listening, seeming mildly irritated which, to me, was perfectly understandable with the inherent pressures of her position. When the announcements were over Dr. N asked me to take her around to visit the classrooms as he had a commitment that had to be kept. I continued the explanation of the project as we started down the hall and, once we were out of sight and earshot of anyone else she abruptly turned to me and hissed through locked jaws, **"What are you doing to help with TEST SCORES?!"**

After recovering from the virtual sucker-punch and assuring myself that this was not a scene from "Invasion of the Body Snatchers" I ticked off my efforts in that area: drilling students on math facts, teaching "test taking skills" in the classrooms, organizing motivational incentives, etc. And then we proceeded with the classroom visits – bubbly, encouraging appearances on her part with bouts of silence in between.

The next day a memo went out to all principals saying that any community projects must be approved by Central Office personnel before implementation and, further, only donations of a check or books could be made by a school to deserving organizations. We were way too far into our toy drive to stop at that point, so we quietly completed the collection (generating more than the required number); organized several carloads of parents, teachers and kids to make the delivery which was received with tearful gratitude; took time to patronize the businesses and restaurants that were functioning primarily out of trailers, and headed home.

After the Christmas break the county's school newsletter came out with a little of this and a little of that, and a nice acknowledgement to some west end schools that had given financial contributions and books to various places during the holiday. My heart sank as I wished that our benevolent families had been recognized. People at "our end of town" usually only received attention for nefarious acts, if at all. But we achieved our goal of sharing the love and our kids experienced the joy of being on the giving end. Mission accomplished. I have a worn, stained, stuffed bunny in a tattered, black gift bag to prove it.

Leadership is a potent combination of strategy and character. But if you must be without one, be without the strategy.
—Gen. H. Norman Schwarzkopf

Up until now I have vehemently defended the majority of teachers and other professionals who comprise that huge, nebulous entity known as The School System. I will always believe that people who are drawn to this field regard it as more of a ministry or calling than just another career. No one expects to come away with fame or fortune. Most educators don't even care about recognition, but they do bristle at unfounded criticism. Within the sanctuary of the classroom, untold miracles occur every day along with unmentionable challenges. Unmentionable, literally, because many a great and gifted educator has brought misery and career termination upon himself or herself as a result of speaking out. Conversely, many an incompetent and even corrupt educator has slid along under the radar for years by keeping the mouth shut or aligning with someone in power. As my husband once said, "The education profession probably has the highest concentration of people with post-graduate degrees but with the least amount to say about how to do their jobs."

Like most bureaucracies in both the public and private sectors, the public school system is similar to a pyramid scheme where people at the top – who are far removed from the daily reality of life in the trenches – earn the most money and call the shots for everyone "below." While there certainly are brilliant, balanced and ethical leaders of corporations, agencies, systems and organizations of all sizes, people who fully comprehend that if not for the worker bees there would be no queen bee, there are also those who see their position of power as a throne-above rather than a pathway-among their people. In the school system, sadly, the only way to achieve promotions and significant salary increases is to leave the classroom and move into administration, a choice that many teachers refuse to make because their passion is direct service to children and youth. Many of those who *are* drawn to administrative roles beyond the local unit are innately turned off by the classroom experience and naturally have difficulty relating to the core, vital, human element of the profession. These are the same people who develop "tests" for measuring good and bad teachers; who support the condemnation of an individual teacher based entirely on student performance. We no longer live in a "Little House on the Prairie" society where one teacher is responsible for everyone in that one-room schoolhouse. Student performance is a result of multiple influences including teams of teachers, transiency from one school to another, home and family experiences and everyone involved in the students' lives up to the point of taking that standardized test.

In perusing the informational sites related to policies, procedures, codes and "best practices" for the system one will invariably discover a lot of legalese along with catchy phrases and objectives, sweeping regulations and metrics for determining success or failure, and swift and severe consequences for stepping outside the box. And yet, in most stories of schools and jurisdictions that have "turned around" there is invariably an individual or group of individuals who did just that – stepped outside the box, analyzed the *specific* needs of a given population and then customized their approach with a focus on the students themselves. What a novel idea, to get to know the school community as people with hopes and doubts, dreams and nightmares, strengths, weaknesses, triumphs and disappointments!

My mind flashes to another scene of a visit by a different

Central Office administrator. I had been summoned to a kindergarten room before the morning bell by a concerned teacher who reported that one of her little boys had been using very profane, sexually-oriented language including the "F-word." She already had suspicions of sexual abuse and asked if I could meet with him to see if I thought he might be in an unsafe situation. I met with him right then, as I had already scheduled an early morning session with a fifth grade boy and his sister who had requested an appointment. All I knew about their issue was that they had been walking down the sidewalk with their cousin when the cousin was shot through the head and killed and nobody would let them talk about the horrific details.

After talking with the kindergarten child I did feel the need to file a report with Child Protective Services so they could further investigate the matter. The school day was now underway and I went back to my office, did some preparation for the session with the siblings, distractedly checked email and then slipped out for a drink of water. Upon hearing the clippety-clip of high heels I turned to see Ms. Winters in her usual high-fashion, snug skirt and jacket, flawless hair and makeup and mildly threatening aura heading toward me. "What are you *doing*?" she asked, with feigned friendliness. In a split second the bits and pieces of her reputation flashed before my eyes: the counselor who lost her job after "documentation" of alleged transgressions, the beloved director who was forced into early retirement when Ms. W wanted someone else in her place, the power-dynamic with the superintendent… What I really wanted to say was, "Well, I'm in between 'F-you' and 'My cousin had his head blown off the other day' " but, instead, I simply said, "Um, I was just checking email…" Her slight gasp and raised, painted eyebrows said it all. I wished I had gone with my initial response (and used the actual word).

What is the toxic elixir that causes some to lose their souls when they achieve positions of power while others seem able to weather the roles with immunity? This is a phenomenon that has always puzzled and intrigued me. From dominant friends to leaders of the world, there seem to be personalities that simply cannot be in charge without seeking total control of everyone else. I suppose that the sociopathic types described in a previous chapter, if they are clever and bright enough to accumulate a lot of letters after their names, are the ones who often end up in positions of authority while the people of character either suck up the pressure out of love for their work or simply go elsewhere. There was a brief spell in my counseling career when I was so chronically outraged by a certain supervisor that I considered leaving the field. A very wise professor listened to me rant for awhile and then simply said, "If you decide to leave, do it because there's something else you really want to do and not because you think another profession is going to be any different." I stayed.

Failing schools and even failing personnel are not "the problem" but, rather, symptoms of a deep and pervasive societal illness. We don't blame and vilify the lump in the breast, the rough patch on the head or the eerie mole; we recognize and even thank those red flags that send us running for answers. We visit doctors, gather information, undergo scans and blood work and do everything in our power to arrive at a diagnosis. Then, with assistance from those who deal with it every day, we proceed to explore whatever has been successful in the past as well as the most current research and state-of-the-art treatments. This is the approach we routinely take for an individual, ill human body, so why are we so reticent to recognize the disastrous impact of an entire society that is clearly wracked with dis-ease? Why must we always take a direct hit before our awareness can shift beyond ourselves to those who are gasping for breath all around us? Ideally, one another's pain should lead to empathy, empathy to compassion, compassion to action, action to the elevation of the human condition, and elevation of the human condition to the "peace on earth" for which we collectively yearn. As Mother Theresa once said, "Not all of us can do great things. But we can do small things with great love."

When I began my school counseling career in 1988 I naively assumed that some kind of agency or department must surely exist as a central clearinghouse of information about state and local, public and private human services. I had worked as a secretary during several sessions of the Virginia General Assembly and saw firsthand how many organizations existed for the purpose of helping others. My counselor role began before the broad commercialization of the internet so I often made phone calls, wrote letters to various government leaders and contacted former legislative associates in search of the director or council that would logically oversee such an effort. It simply did not exist and, as far as I know, still does not exist twenty-six years later. No one is connecting the dots. Well-meaning groups both large and small are constantly re-inventing the wheel, staking their claims on little piecemeal territories and spending a whole lot of money that never gets audited or efficiently directed to those whom they purport to serve.

Even as this book comes to completion a new, "statewide school division" has been considered in Virginia to "rehab failing schools." A local newspaper described the goal of the group as an effort to "seize control of schools that have failed to meet basic academic benchmarks for four years in a row." Whether this comes to pass in some form or another or not, hear those words: seize control. This is the language of despots, not the wisdom of healers. Virginia also plans to bring the "Teach for America" program to our capital city – a well-intentioned organization that integrates professionals with minimal teacher training into public schools – in spite of the hundreds of unemployed, fully certified teachers statewide who would love to give it a shot. I once chuckled at the adage, "The beatings will continue until morale improves" – but it has become less and less amusing with time.

Two retired colleagues, one of whom still substitutes within the system, invited me for lunch recently. We reminisced about past experiences, laughed, shed a few tears and cherished the memories of widespread, collaborative efforts on behalf of kids and families over the years. The one who is still plugged into the grid looked contemplative. "That can't happen anymore," she said. "Now the teachers must conform to the 'Best Practices' as ordained by the Department of Education. The school day is divided into very clearly defined modules with designated amounts of time to cover specific material. They can't allow the kids to ask questions or explore concepts unless there is time left over after the information is disseminated." I asked what the counselors are doing now. She just looked sad and I knew the answer, because it was already beginning to happen before I left in 2003 – they become just another warm body in the school to organize schedules, facilitate meetings, shuffle papers and help raise test scores. She also said that elementary school children in Virginia no longer study the United States of America as a nation; neither the geography nor the overall history. They might study our own state and those surrounding it, but they no longer look at a map of the country and learn about the states, the capitals, the industries, the people. But at least they know about Egypt and the pharaohs.

The greatest tragedy about the public school system is that the ridiculous politics, problems, power struggles and personality conflicts ultimately trickle down to the most vulnerable and trusting among us; the children, who depend upon us to model good character, critical thinking skills and a lifelong love of learning. The children, to whom we pass the baton of leadership – a sobering and frightening thought.

What can I do?

- If your state or locality allows election rather than appointment of School Board members, pay attention and let your vote speak! The board actually does have a significant "say" in important matters such as the hiring of superintendents who ultimately set the tone. Even when appointed, candidates should be qualified to make decisions that impact schools and communities. Participate in the vetting process as much as possible.
- Become a trustworthy advocate for teachers. Private citizens can freely express concerns while school employees truly cannot. Be a respected, public voice for change whenever possible.
- If you *are* a school employee, read your contract thoroughly until you fully understand the legal protections and possible repercussions of speaking out about the needs of your situation.
- Always assume there is more than one side to any story and, if you have the time and the inclination, investigate! Social media has its pitfalls but can also be a tremendously helpful tool in digging up the facts.
- Nothing kills quality control like political correctness. Whether you are a school employee, a parent, a volunteer or simply a concerned citizen, substantiated information about the incompetency of someone in the system should be *reported*. Begin by going through the proper channels, but if all else fails remember that no organization likes bad publicity. Knowledge is power, and so is the truth.

Chapter 10
Racists, Pimps and Carpetbaggers

One of the saddest lessons of history is this: If we've been bamboozled long enough, we tend to reject any evidence of the bamboozle. We're no longer interested in finding out the truth. The bamboozle has captured us. It's simply too painful to acknowledge, even to ourselves, that we've been taken. Once you give a charlatan power over you, you almost never get it back.

—Carl Sagan

Gigantic, popcorn clouds adorn the azure sky as volunteers scamper around the school grounds with maps, highway cones, mysteriously shaped bags full of equipment, tables for audio apparatus and refreshments. The excitement is palpable as class after class files out in brightly colored team shirts; they've been practicing for this in various ways all year. It's Field Day – a day when "competition" is not a dirty word but a delicious challenge to be the very best at something; to experience the thrill of success and learn the grace of good sportsmanship in defeat. Everyone is still and silent as the gym teacher reminds them of the rules of the day, the flag is saluted and the Star Spangled Banner blasts through the speakers followed by an explosion of applause and cheers as the kids head to their posts.

This isn't just any Field Day – it's *every* Field Day at schools across the nation. These aren't just our kids, they're *all* kids – a microcosm of humanity: the thin and the heavy, the child with the bald head and prosthetic leg along with the high-speed runner, the Down Syndrome child who runs in the wrong direction but is gently turned around and cheered on by his teammates, the budding athletes and the klutzes. I gaze out across the beautiful faces; the impossible, subtle shades of skin pigmentation, and recall the refrain of a popular "Up With People" song from the '60s: *What color is God's skin? What color is God's skin? I said it's black, brown, it's yellow; it is red and it is white. Everyone's the same in the good Lord's sight* (© Thomas Wilkes and David Stevenson). We church-goers do a lot of talking, praying and singing about the "kingdom of God" as if it exists somewhere in the great beyond; as if God is some little old man with a white beard who will give us a thumbs up or down when we cross over. But this is it, before my eyes. Everything we say we hope for, die for, govern for and pray for – peace on earth, love of neighbor, a return to innocence – it's all here.

Like transparent, pictorial overlays in the old science and anatomy books, scenes of humanity at its finest are layered in our psyches if we would but take the time to flip through the pages within: snapshots of the hugs, laughter and indiscernible languages at an airport; the shared grief at visitation time before the funeral of a loved one; the strength and unity of a city in crisis, and the fortitude of those who assist; the Olympics. Every day we are offered opportunities to observe and celebrate our human connection, and yet there have always been those among us whose mission is to divide and conquer; to not only emphasize our differences but to capitalize upon them for personal gain. Somehow these people inevitably end up in positions of leadership and convince us that that their wisdom and integrity is beyond reproach.

So who are the racists, pimps and carpetbaggers in our

society, and how does their influence affect education? There are many definitions and explanations for these three terms, both literal and metaphorical, but "racism" is fairly universally defined as "discrimination or prejudice based on race." The word "pimp" could broadly refer to someone who benefits financially by forcing others, through fear, abuse or intimidation, to perform acts that violate their human dignity in exchange for basic survival. And while "carpetbaggers" were Northerners who headed south after the Civil War to take unfair advantage of the unstable economy and societal turbulence, the word also refers in general to those who exploit the vulnerable and the trusting to augment their own wealth or power. Within the framework of these three descriptions are way too many examples, unfortunately, of people who have lost the capacity for love, compassion or empathy and cannot see beyond their own egos or legacy. And I do believe the capacity is "lost" versus "nonexistent" – these qualities are part of our DNA and always retrievable as demonstrated throughout history. In fact, few stories are more inspiring than those of despicable lives turned around to become beacons of light for others. For example, one of the most beloved hymns for more than two centuries has been "Amazing Grace", written in 1773 by English poet and clergyman John Newton, a former slave trader who wrote it as a message of God's forgiveness and redemption to all who felt lost to sin. Where there is life, there is hope; and where there is hope, there is potential for peace on earth.

As a white elementary school counselor with a majority of black students, I loved Black History Month. It was a time to recognize the accomplishments, inventions, writings and *courage* of so many people whose lives could serve as models for the students. One of the black teachers – a dear friend and a blessing to every student ever in her charge – gave me dozens of brief write-ups on outstanding black Americans to read each morning during the announcements. Not only were these summaries educational and inspiring; they also brought to life real people who had often overcome tremendous odds, survived unbelievable challenges and made invaluable contributions to society in art, music, literature, science, technology, engineering and mathematics. All of the children enjoyed the daily anecdotes and the black children in particular held their heads a little higher as these were *their* people; their true superheroes. If only we could have protected them from the outside world where, unfortunately, all too many people were determined to keep them stuck in the past. While the European/African slave trade was a collaborative crime of both Europeans *and* Africans; and while the Abolitionist movement was successful due to the combined moral indignation and enterprise of blacks *and* whites; and while people of African and Caucasian heritage have been loving, marrying, procreating and working side by side and hand in hand for centuries, there are those of all shades who would have us believe that white-equals-bad and black-equals-good in every circumstance and that none of the other races or cultures matter as much.

Yes, racism abounds around the globe and there is no such thing as "reverse racism." Racists are racists and they come in all colors. There always have been and always will be ignorant haters who refuse to acknowledge the value of anyone different from themselves. There are "good guys" and "bad guys" in every race, every society, every business; even in our faith communities where love should be the universal message. And like the notorious Nurse Ratched from Ken Keysey's classic, *One Flew Over the Cuckoo's Nest*, there are leaders who maintain their positions of power by keeping others down; by making sure those who show signs of hopeful, independent thinking are instantly reminded of the wounds and iniquities of the past; of their "need" for someone to tell them what to do and of their obligation to tow the line and think as one mind. The same ideologues who want to "seize control of failing schools" also speak of "the black vote, the gay vote, the Latino vote, the Catholic vote..." as if these compartmentalized humans share a collective brain that must be constantly manipulated and controlled. Is this not similar to "pimping" – making a fine living off of the huddled masses who have been brainwashed into believing they can't do any better? Are these artificially defined clusters not made up of unique individuals whose empowerment would, in the long run, more effectively improve the lives of the entire group? While it is true that those who do not know history are destined to repeat it, what purpose does it serve to perseverate only upon the most despicable, unjust elements when, in fact, the greatest stories of triumph also emerge from those very dark periods in time? Shouldn't history be studied with a clear, balanced, wide-angle lens depicting the continuous battles between good and evil? Is it dishonest to be proud of how far we have all come together as Americans even as we strive to improve?

And then there are those who swoop in during times of incredible distress and confusion with promises of assistance, restoration and commitment to full investigation of a given situation, only to run off with the money and misplaced trust of people who believed in them. These are the carpetbaggers and they can be cleverly disguised as anything from contractors to local leaders to heads of government to ministers of God. The damage they do to the human spirit far outweighs any physical destruction. Nobody likes to believe they've been bamboozled and when it becomes undeniable the feelings of betrayal turn into anger, anger to despair, and despair to resignation which is fuel for the fire of those who thrive on control.

At the risk of creating backlash, I must speak the truth that even at the elementary school level it is not "cool" to be a smart black boy. The cruel myth is perpetuated throughout the school years, too often by *black* leaders and "role models" with the not-always-subtle message that it is "acting white" to aspire to fame, fortune, white collar professionalism, academic prominence or traditional family values. Excuse me? What is the message there, that only white people are capable and deserving of happiness and success? How confusing for the hard-working, black community of parents who are encouraging their kids to strive for the American dream. Even at the elementary school level it is all too often acceptable for black children to call one another "niggers" and use disparaging words against other races with impunity. Where are they hearing this kind of hate-speak and learning that these skewed life priorities are the norm? Primarily from the contemporary heroes of the entertainment industry along with athletes, politicians and "religious leaders" whose shameful examples are not being counter-balanced at home or in school. *All* children are profoundly affected by these negative influences, albeit subconsciously, and thus we see the rise in bullying behaviors and total lack of self-respect or even the most basic self-awareness. The second "greatest commandment" is to love our neighbors as ourselves. I believe the problem is that we *do*... our love of neighbor reflects exactly how we love ourselves, which apparently isn't much.

At a medical dinner many years ago our guest speaker was a handsome, articulate black physician who had risen above a treacherous childhood in the projects of an inner city. When he sat down beside me to eat I expressed my enthusiasm for his life story and asked if he ever went back to his old neighborhood to speak at schools or community functions. He actually looked startled and said bluntly, "NO! Nobody wants to go back once they get out of that kind of an environment!" I told him I thought it could really help a lot of kids if they met someone from their own city who had become so successful and he said they would figure out how to do it just as he had. And then he simply changed the subject.

Now, many people *do* go back and extend a long arm with a hand-up to those who simply cannot find their way out, and whenever it happens there are powerful, positive ripple effects that emanate for miles and years. While it is exemplary and honorable to reach out internationally – building schools in under-developed countries, sending financial aid, adopting babies and providing medical and educational resources – it would also be wonderful if people of wealth, means and recognition would funnel some of that passion to our own kids who are hungry, cold, abused, illiterate and desperately in need of every kind of affirmative attention. There's a reason why, at the beginning of every airline flight, the instructions are to put the oxygen mask on yourself first; so that you are then able to help the ones closest to you and they in turn can help the ones closest to them, and so on until everyone can survive. It all boils down to personal responsibility; to *true* love of neighbor.

So the racists, pimps and carpetbaggers are among us and sometimes they are us. If we have ever turned our nose up at someone because of the outer appearance, or ever profited from "using" people in a way that diminished their humanity, or ever taken unfair advantage of people who trusted us during a tumultuous time in their lives then we are as guilty as the most corrupt and prominent figures that we love to hold in contempt. Recently a very highly respected and wealthy black celebrity, once considered an icon of inclusion and spiritual enlightenment, was asked to share her thoughts on racism. After acknowledging the value of understanding American history as a pathway to creating a better future she remarked, "...I said this for my own, you know, community in the south – there are still generations of people, older people, who were born and bred and marinated in it, in that prejudice and racism, and they just have to die."

This is insulting and even dangerous thinking on many levels. First of all it implies that prejudice and racism are the transgressions of one particular generation, ostensibly white, and once they're dead and gone the country will have a universal "Free at last!" kind of moment. It suggests that the damaging, elitist views of racists belong to "somebody else" and are not recycled generation after generation, from womb to tomb, by people of all colors from all walks of life. How disappointing. And how discouraging for those who teach the children, optimistically clinging to the belief that such crippling attitudes will surely turn a corner soon and eventually there will actually be a color blind society.

I was a child of the 1950s and '60s. I, along with millions of others, raised my voice in prayer and my fist in determination for equal and civil rights for all people. I wept at the senseless death of Dr. Martin Luther King, Jr. who clearly envisioned a brave, new world for the descendants of slaves. I wrote letters to newspapers while other youth were smoking pot and dropping out. I volunteered with disadvantaged kids, became a teacher, stayed at home to raise my own kids and then became an elementary school counselor *always* with a focus on building a better society. I was raised by parents who did not tolerate the disrespectful treatment of anyone; whose home was known almost as a halfway-house for all of our strange and quirky friends who might not have been welcomed anywhere else. We offered humble gratitude for all who served our country, attended Mass every Sunday and took seriously the stories of the man Jesus who hung out with the dregs of society in defiance of the racists and elitists of *His* day. I may vehemently disagree with people at times – in fact, I may not even like certain people at all – but it will never be because of the color of their skin. When the race shills cry "Racist!" every time someone disagrees with a person of color they dilute the pool of *true* racists who are the bane of civilization, making them much more difficult to spot. They silence the conversations that urgently need to happen in a free society and they paralyze the efforts of good people who are trying to move forward together as un-hyphenated Americans. They are the single, greatest threat to the survival of "the land of the free and the home of the brave."

In this great but admittedly flawed United States of America, who is "purely" anything? Do we no longer pride ourselves on our unique "melting pot" status in the world? On a larger scale, considering the many millennia of people conquering people, assimilating, being assimilated, seeding the globe with their traditions, genetic bouquets and perspectives, who is purely anything *anywhere*? Just because someone's ancestor from Africa introduced dark pigmentation to the skin at some point, does that define the person as "black"? Does my northern European heritage pigeon-hole me as exclusively "white"? Through genetic tracking I have discovered ancient ancestral ties to northern Africa, Eastern Asia and Native America! How fabulous! I've learned to beware of those who are obsessed with their own skin color because they are invariably also obsessed with everyone else's. How many people actually know what their specific forbears were doing during all the trials and tribulations of humanity throughout the ages? Does it ever occur to the race-fixated, the pimps and the carpetbaggers described above that in 21st century America a huge percentage of the population is *multi*-racial? Or that children love the people who love them – whether black, white, Asian, Hispanic, Native American or all of the above whether biologically or simply legally related to them? Do the hate-speakers ever consider how much pain and inner conflict they wreak upon people of all ages by demanding that they choose sides *within themselves* whenever they insult, demean, criticize or condemn those who skin tone is different from their own? Evidently not. Will it ever end?

At the end of a long school day I was taking a break in the teacher's lounge with a few amiable colleagues and we started sharing funny stories about our own children. One of the teachers offered that her daughter, as a little girl, loved to go fishing with her daddy and then help with the delicious fish-fry later at home. One day she caught the most magnificent fish she had ever seen, its scales shimmering like little rainbows, its tail swishing and sparkling like spun silver. She could not imagine this treasure enduring a common, brutal death upon the cutting board so she slipped it out of the pile and hid it in the basement. Time passed, and the family began to notice an unpleasant odor wafting up from below. The little girl could not come forward with the truth, so ashamed was she about her little secret and devastated about the fate of her prized catch. Finally the smell became overwhelming and a painstaking search by the family ended at the rotting, stinking, bony carcass so carefully hidden away.

When the laughter died down among our little group I thought, *Wow... there's a meaningful message in there somewhere about what happens when we try to hide the truth... it eventually reveals itself one way or another... sometimes it has to really stink to get our attention... there's a life metaphor in there... or maybe the title of a book...* Thanks, Edna!

What can we do?

- Begin with honest introspection. Re-read the expanded definitions of "racists, pimps and carpetbaggers" and think about times when those terms could describe your own attitudes and behavior. Become mindful of "...the beam in your own eye." (Matt 7:3)
- Be courageous – literally walk away from racist or demeaning humor, forms of theft that may be legal but not moral, and manipulative schemes that take unfair advantage of anyone anywhere. Strive to set a good example.
- Read the poem "If" by Rudyard Kipling and take it to heart. My father had it memorized and shared it often. Remember it during those times when you realize you have been "bamboozled" and then move forward with dignity.
- Explore your DNA and celebrate *your own* diversity! This will help you to truly celebrate the diversity of others.
- Teach a child about real-life superheroes – both historical and current. Hit the "restart" button for the next generation.

Chapter 11
Inspiration

How wonderful that no one need wait a single moment to improve the world.

—Anne Frank

Walking along the ocean at sunrise, I unabashedly welcome the sensory pleasures of the new day: firm, wet sand under my feet... the moist, salty breeze... dolphin fins mysteriously arching and disappearing into the surf... pelicans gliding in uncanny precision just above the water line... the plaintive calling of the gulls... the impossible variations of pink and yellow morphing across the horizon. I thank God for this time of inspiration, and immediately wish I could bring a bus load of students here.

It happens every time. From visits to the mountains, to a simple lovely tune, I think of the children whose spirits are rarely lifted to that state of ecstasy known as inspiration. They come from all walks of life, crossing all socioeconomic lines. Even the materially wealthy cannot appreciate the fascinating dance of God's miracles if no one has ever taught them to set ego aside and view the world through immortal eyes. But the privileged do have more opportunities for inspiration, albeit inadvertent at times. They tend to go more places, have connections with more people and read or be-read-to more often.

Woe to the little ones whose lives are steeped in fear, grief or poverty; who go from dull, inadequate homes to dull, inadequate schools day after day. Too often, these children's perspective of the world is worse than sad; worse than the confined yard of the fenced-in dog. It is emotionally flat. Loved ones live and die, come and go as regularly as the rising and setting sun, and their hearts learn to be wary of joy and peace.

And who can fault them? Their inability to trust is not some self-centered, whiney wish that the world would drop everything and "understand" them. It is borne of dashed hopes and accumulated disappointments that create a layer of psychological scar tissue between their tender, inner core and the world outside.

The frequent low achievement of such children is not a manifestation of limited intellect, but limited experience. Educators may do everything possible to compensate for the void, but if the support and stimulation do not continue beyond the classroom these children may always be swimming upstream – making progress, but rarely leading the group.

The cool water rushes over my feet, washing away the accumulated sand with each step. Every cleansing is a fresh start. But eventually I must cross the vast stretch of hot sand to reach the comforts of the civilized world. Will there be fresh water to relieve the burning skin? Will this momentary peace sustain me during difficult times ahead? Will brief, daily respites and second chances provide enough spiritual rejuvenation for the children to confront the grim tasks of daily living?

I think of the contemporary parable of a man plucking dying starfish from the unforgiving terrain and tossing them back into the surf. As the story goes, someone comes along and cynically says, "You can't save them all." The man quietly picks up another one, flings it into the water with a satisfied expression and replies simply, "…saved that one." I turn the children over to God, over and over and over. And I imagine hearing Him say occasionally, "…saved that one."

www.ingramcontent.com/pod-product-compliance
Lightning Source LLC
Chambersburg PA
CBHW022113090426
42743CB00008B/825